JULY 2022

AN ANTHOLOGY OF ARTICLES

BRAIN BOOSTER ARTICLES

Copyright © Brain Booster Articles
All Rights Reserved.

This book has been published with all efforts taken to make the material error-free after the consent of the author. However, the author and the publisher do not assume and hereby disclaim any liability to any party for any loss, damage, or disruption caused by errors or omissions, whether such errors or omissions result from negligence, accident, or any other cause.

While every effort has been made to avoid any mistake or omission, this publication is being sold on the condition and understanding that neither the author nor the publishers or printers would be liable in any manner to any person by reason of any mistake or omission in this publication or for any action taken or omitted to be taken or advice rendered or accepted on the basis of this work. For any defect in printing or binding the publishers will be liable only to replace the defective copy by another copy of this work then available.

Contents

Preface

"Start writing, no matter what. The water does not flow until the faucet is turned on".

-Louis L'Amour

This book is a bouquet of articles contributed by students, professors and academicians. Hundreds of students and professors are contributing their work to Brain Booster Articles, we are here to provide ample information about Law and Contemporary issues. Our aim is to provide a platform for today's generation to express their views and ideas on law and contemporary law.

PROTECTION OF CHILDREN FROM SEXUAL OFFENCES ACT

Author: Harsh Srivastava, II year of B.A.,LL.B. from University of Petroleum and Energy Studies

Introduction

Children are intended to be protected from all forms of sexual abuse by the Protection of Children from Sexual Offences Act, 2012 (the "POCSO

Act, 2012"). Even though the United Nations ratified the Convention on the Rights of the Child in 1989, India did not pass any legislation to address crimes against children until 2012. It stipulates severe penalties for crimes against children, ranging from the death penalty in cases of extreme penetrative sexual assault to a minimum sentence of 20 years in jail.

Neccesity of POSCO Act

India has one of the greatest populations of children in the world; according to census data from 2011, there are 472 million children in India who are under the age of eighteen. According to a broad interpretation of Article 21 of the Indian Constitution, citizens are guaranteed the state's protection of children, and it is also required given that India is a party to the UN Convention on the Rights of the Child. The Goa Children's Act, 2003 was the sole particular law addressing child abuse prior to the POCSO Act's enactment.

The following sections of the Indian Penal Code dealt with child sexual abuse:

- I.P.C. (1860) 375- Rape
- I.P.C. (1860) 354- Outraging the modesty of a woman
- I.P.C. (1860) 377- Unnatural offences

The IPC, however, was not able to properly safeguard the child due to a number of flaws, including:

Male victims or anybody else are not shielded from sexual acts of penetration other than "conventional" peno-vaginal intercourse per IPC 375.

There is no statutory definition of "modesty" in IPC 354. It is a compoundable offence that has a light penalty. Additionally, it does not safeguard a boy's "modesty."

The phrase "unnatural offences" is not defined in IPC 377. It is not intended to criminalise the sexual exploitation of children and only applies to victims who have been penetrated by their attacker's sex act.

As a result, it was necessary to change the law with a focus on a child protection legislation.

POCSO Act's scope

The POCSO Act, 2012 is not the only piece of legislation in India that addresses issues of child sexual abuse. The provisions of the Code of Criminal Procedure, 1973, Indian Penal Code, 1860, Juvenile Justice Act, and Information Technology Act, 2000 overlap, encompass the process, and describe the offences, hence the POCSO Act cannot be considered a comprehensive code in and of itself.

Importance of the Act

The POCSO Act, 2012 was passed at a time when reports of child sexual abuse were on the rise. It outlines the process for putting these laws into effect and includes rules for protecting children from sexual assault and pornography.

Minors's safety is never guaranteed anyplace because incidents of sexual abuse against children happen at schools, churches, parks, hostels, and other public areas. With such new threats, it was important to pass separate legislation that might offer a solid framework for reducing the frequency of such offences and punishing those who commit them.

The Act has been crucial in establishing a strong judicial system for those who have been sexually abused and in highlighting the importance of children's rights and protection .

Features of the POCSO Act, 2012

- Identity of the victim must be kept confidential under Section 23 of the POCSO Act, which also imposes a requirement to do so unless the Special Court has authorised disclosure. No reports in the medium may reveal a child's identify, including his name, residence, portrait, family information, school, neighbourhood, or any other details that could reveal the child's identity, according to Section 23(2). The Calcutta High Court repeated the law created under Section 23 and ruled that anyone, including a police officer, shall be prosecuted if they commit such a breach in the landmark case of Bijoy Guddu Das v. The State of West Bengal (2017).

- Mandatory reporting of child abuse cases: Because of the stigma associated with these crimes, elders try to conceal sexual abuse cases that occur behind closed doors. Therefore, Sections 19 to 22 of the POCSO Act have made reporting of these instances by third parties who have knowledge of or suspicion of such offences necessary for the proper enforcement of the POCSO Act. These regulations were created with the presumption that because children are defenceless and helpless, society has a responsibility to safeguard their interests.

- The last seen theory: In cases involving child sexual abuse, the last seen theory is used. In accordance with this hypothesis, when there is a very small amount of time between when someone was last seen alive and when they were last seen with the victim, it is assumed that they are the ones who committed the crime. It was noted in the 2012 case of Shyamal Ghosh v. State of West Bengal that it is unreasonable for the courts to use the last seen approach when there is a significant time lapse.

- Investigation and trial procedures that are child-friendly are outlined in Sections 24, 26, and 33 of the POCSO Act. These sections outline the investigation and trial process that has been designed with the requirements of a child in mind.

The question of whether Section 155(2) of the Code of Criminal Procedure will apply to the investigation of an offence under Section 23 of the Protection of Children from Sexual Offenses Act, 2012 was recently decided inconclusively by a two-judge Supreme Court panel (POCSO).

A police officer must have a magistrate's approval before conducting an investigation under Section 155(2) of the Criminal Procedure Code. The offence of disclosing the identify of the victim of a sexual offence is covered by Section 23 of the POCSO.

<u>What problems arise when children are sexually abused?</u>

Child sexual abuse is a multifaceted issue that has an adverse effect on children's physical safety, mental health, well-being, and behavioural characteristics.

Amplification Resulting from digital technologies: The exploitation and abuse of children has increased as a result of mobile and digital technology. Online bullying, harassment, and child pornography are just a few of the newer types of child abuse that have arisen.

Effectiveness of the Law: The Protection of Children against Sexual Offences Act of 2012 (POCSO Act) was passed by the Government of India, although it has not succeeded in preventing sexual abuse of children.

There are several explanations for this. Low Conviction Rate: If one averages the last five years, the rate of convictions under the POCSO statute is just about 32%, and 90% of the cases are still pending.

Despite the POCSO Act's explicit requirement that the trial and conviction process be completed in one year, it took 16 months for the primary accused in the Kathua Rape case to be found guilty.

Unfriendly to Children: Difficulties with determining the child's age. Particularly rules that prioritise biological age rather than mental age.

<u>Reference</u>

1 . https://vikaspedia.in/education/policies-and-schemes/protection-of-children-from-sexual-offences-act

2 .POCSO Act, 2012, Section 3

3 . Section 5.

4. Section 7

5. POCSO Act, Section 19(6)

<u>Author's Bio</u>

Harsh Srivastava belongs from Varanasi (Benaras is older than history, older than tradition, older even than legend and looks twice as old as all of them put together - Mark Twain) . Currently pursuing BA LLB from University of Petroleum and Energy Studies, Dehradun . His interest is not only in the field of literature but also in the field of music ,photography , dance and event management. Multitasking child with full of creativity and patience

CHAPTER TWO

HOW TO GET A GUN LICENSE IN INDIA

Author: Abhinav Pandey, I year of B.A.,LL.B.(Hons.) from University of Lucknow

<u>Introductions to Arms License</u>

What is License?

A Arms License is also Known as License or Gun License permit issued by a government authority typically by the police, that allows the licensee to buy, own, possess, or carry a arm, often subject to a number of conditions or restrictions, especially with regard to storage requirements or the completion of a firearms safety course, as well as background checks, etc.

The permit or license scope varies according to what fire arms or activity it allows the holder to legally do with the firearm. Some jurisdictions may require a firearm license to own a firearm, to engage in target shooting or collecting, or to carry a concealed firearm, or operate a business such as being a gun dealer or a gunsmith. Some jurisdictions may require separate licenses for shotguns, or rifles

The guns in India are strictly regulated by the law. The Arms act 1959 along with the Arms rules 1962 provides for all the provisions regarding the sale, manufacture, acquisition, import-export transport of arms and ammunition unless a license which is difficult to obtain.

History of Gun License

It is a very interesting fact in history that the Arms Act was introduced by British Raj in 1878 to limit the sale, manufacture and use of arms and ammunition so to suppress the rebellion by Indian rebels because the people then especially in part of Rajasthan had the knowledge of metal extraction and making arms out of them could be a possible future risk for the British. Later, the Act was amended and reintroduced in1959 after independence.

Issuing of Gun License

Chapter III of the Arms Rules, 2016 specifies the special categories of a license, or we can say specifies the reason for which the license can be issued:

Section 35:

Licence for Destruction of Wild Animals which do injury to Human Beings or Cattle and Damage to Crops

Section 36:

Licence for Training and Target Practice .

Section 37:

Licence for Sport Shooting Association.

Section 38:

Licence for Shooting Ranges.

Section 39:

Licence for Accredited Trainers.

Section 40:

Quantity of Ammunition to Sports Persons, Shooting Associations, etc.

Section 41:

Licence to Museums.

ELIGIBILITY

- He or She Must Be ACitizen of India And Must Show The Identification Documents While Applying For A Gun License
- He or She Should Have Completed At Least 21 Years Of Age.

PROCEDURE TO BE FOLLOWED

The person applying for the license must be of minimum 21 years of age. The applicant has to fill an application and pay a prescribed fee. Certain documents are required to be attached with the application like:

1.Date of Birth Proof

2.Aadhar Card

3.Identification Proof

4.Residence Proof

5.VoterID card or Passport or Pan Card or Identification document issued for employees with a declaration in the form of an affidavit

6.Medical Certificate for Both mental and physical fitness

7.Education qualification, in case of professionals

After the submission of the License form the licensing authority calls for an enquiry report prepared by the incharge of the nearest police station. The report is supposed to be submitted within the prescribed time. A strict background check up takes place about the background of the person, family and neighbours are interviewed about the behaviour of that person. His Physical and Mental health is also checked. The person undergoes a personal interview where he is supposed to state the purpose for which he has applied for the license and then the report is sent to the National Crime Record Bureau for record-keeping.So once the whole process is over and therefore the investigating officer is satisfied that the person won't use the open for the other purpose then the mentioned one then the person gets the approval but getting an approval doesn't mean that an individual can now get the weapon in hand. Now, after the Arms license, the customer obviously possesses to contact the dealer for the procurement of the gun. For this, the customer will be got to book a preorder to urge the gun from any licensed shop of their choice

<u>DOCUMENTS REQUIRED FOR GETTING THE GUN FROM FACTORY</u>

1.One Copy of the Non-Objection Certificate for the Owner of the factory and one copy of Non-Objection Certificate for the Police authorities. just in case if the Arms license is valid across whole India then no Non-Objection Certificate is required.

2.Issued License with Place and Valid Date.

3.There is also a requirement for the transport license of the place where the factory is found.

<u>REFUSAL TO LICENSE</u>

To be prohibited by this Act or by any law for the non effective from acquiring, having in his possession or carrying any arms or ammunition, or to be of unsound mind, or the person is found unfit for a licence or where the licensing authority deems it necessary for the security of the overall public peace or for public safety to refuse to grant such licence.

HOW TO SELL YOUR LICENSED GUN

If somebody wants to sell their weapon they should submit an application with 5Rs Court Stamp on it with attached copy of the original Arm license and inform the Arms Branch that they're interested in selling their weapon.they should provide all the documents which they earlier submitted for getting the weapons issued.

CAN THE GUN BE TRANSFERRED?

If the Original Arm license is present during the lifetime of the person who wants to transfer the ownership of the Gun to the legal heirs by making application on a plain paper and this paper will be attached with the A Form of the person to whom the transfer of license is given.If the original license has expired, then the application can be made again in the A form . There will be the requirement of passport size photos and there should be no objection from the legal heirs.

AREA VALIDITY OF ARMS LICENCES

The state governments have been advised to allow area validity upto a maximum of three adjoining States and also to consider AIV requests at State level for the following categories:

1.Sitting Union Ministers

2.Sitting Members of Parliament

3.Officers of All India Services

4.Personnel of Military and Para-Military

For the applicants not covered by the above categories, the State Government shall seek prior concurrence of Ministry of Home Affairs with full clarification in deserving cases. All India Validity can be allowed for three years in such cases and shall be re-considered after Three years by the State Government with prior concurrence of Ministry of Home Affairs. The State Government may send data of All-India validity on quarterly basis to Ministry of Home Affairs.

REFRENCES

1.Wikepedia

2.Articles

3. https://www.thehindu.com

4. https://blog.ipleaders.in

5.Oxford English Dictionary

<u>Author's Bio</u>

Abhinav Pandey is someone who is constantly Excited and ready for the next chapter of his Life. He is contemporary But compassionate Writer who trise to infuse his work with a wide range of experience, And ideas. He enjoys Being able to make His writing relatable to others by generalizing The ideas he is writing About.

AN ANALYSIS OF INSANITY AS A DEFENCE UNDER CRIMINAL LAW

Author: Manisha Bharathi R, III year of B.B.A.,LL.B. from Symbiosis Law School, Hyderabad

Abstract

Insanity, derived in the 16th century, from the Latin word 'insanitas' or 'insanus', means unhealthfulness with respect to the mind. This piece of study focuses upon the theme of insanity as a defence under Criminal Law. The paper entails the various essentials necessary to constitute insanity and the various rules and tests available and used widely in order to confirm the applicability of insanity as a defence in particular scenarios. The first chapter in the article talks about the origin of this defence and how it has evolved for the modern times. The second chapter primarily gives out the factors of differentiation between medical insanity and legal insanity and then goes on to elucidate the characteristics required for legal insanity. The paper, then, entails a brief elucidation regarding the theory of diminished responsibility and the concept of being guilty but mentally ill. Further, the paper contains a description of the situation and judgment delivered in landmark cases relating to insanity in India. Additionally, the paper delves into a comparative aspect and explains the rules and tests for insanity as a defence under UK and US laws in comparison to what is prevalent in India.

Introduction

Insanity can be defined under law as a disturbed or unsound state of mind that renders a person devoid of the mental capacity required to do an act, enter an agreement, authorise something etc.[i] This unsound state of mind allows the person an exemption from civil or criminal liability, which is why it is termed as defence of insanity under law. This logic is deduced from the legal maxim: "furiosus solo furore punitur", which means that a mad man is punished by his madness alone and does not attract civil or criminal responsibility for his acts. The maxim of "Actus Non Facit Reum Nisi Mens Sit Rea" also finds application here. It means that an act does not find a person liable if the person does not possess a guilty mind. Guilty mind (Mens Rea) i.e., a blameworthy mental condition is an important element to constitute a crime and that will be lacking in a person with an unsound mind as he/ she is not aware of the nature of the act done or whether it is right or wrong. On the same lines is the maxim of "Furiosi Nulla Voluntas Est" which means that a mad man lacks free will. In law, this maxim can be interpreted as that "there must be as an essential ingredient in a criminal offence, some blameworthy condition of mind, and such condition of mind cannot justly be imputed to madmen who are under a natural disability of distinguishing between good and evil."[ii]

From the criminal aspect, Section 84 of the Indian Penal Code (IPC) talks about the defence of insanity. It states that "Nothing is an offence which is done by a person who, at the time of doing it, by reason of unsoundness of mind, is incapable of knowing the nature of the act, or that he is doing what is either wrong or contrary to law."[iii] It is peculiar to note that this statute does not use the word 'insanity' but instead uses the phrase 'unsoundness of mind' which indicates insanity of mind.

Insanity as a defence in Indian law (Section 84 of the IPC) has M'Naughten's Rule as its origin/ backing. For the application of the defence of insanity, it is necessary that two essentials be qualified:

- The accused must have been in an unsound state of mind during the commission of the act.
- The accused must not have known/ was incapable of knowing the nature of the act committed by him/ her.
- He/ She must not have known or was incapable of knowing that the act committed was wrong or contrary to the law.

Section 84 of the IPC has not undergone any change since its inception. However, an attempt was made by the Law Commission of India in 1971, via its 42nd report to revisit the provision but no changes were inflicted. When it comes to the usage of this defence, burden of proof lies wholly with the defendant and the insanity or unsoundness of mind has to be proved beyond reasonable doubt. This paper will delve into the essentials for the use of the defence of insanity, tests and theories used in relation to it, its position in criminal law and the prominence of the defence in the US and the UK law along with the Indian scenario.

<u>Literature Review</u>

Randy Borum and Solomon M. Fulero, in their journal article, "Empirical Research on the Insanity Defense and Attempted Reforms: Evidence Toward Informed Policy"[iv] clearly explain the application of the defence in criminal law. The authors state that the two important components to establish a crime are actus reus (action) and mens rea (intent). They also state that it is a general assumption that people act on their own, free will and are responsible for their acts. The defence of insanity, however, comes in as a defence at this juncture because the person committing the act can be affected by a mental illness which in turn affects his/ her cognitive abilities to an extent that it does not constitute the real intent and free will of that person. This state of being exempts the person from criminal responsibility for his/ her act. Further, the article goes on to explain that the widely used insanity defence standards are the M'Naghten Rules and the provisions of the Model Penal Code. The article explores various perceptions and misconceptions regarding the use of the said defence, tests for its application, usage in murder cases etc.

Richard J. Bonnie, in his journal article, "The Moral Basis of the Insanity Defense"[v] particularly focuses on the importance of the availability of the insanity defence and why the burden of proof should be on the defendant/ accused. Further, the author analyses various tests and theories relating to the defence and states that a test of insanity, to decide on the exemption of liability for a mentally unsound person who has committed a crime, must focus on the accused's "ability to appreciate the wrongfulness of his conduct."[vi]

In the book "Ratanlal and Dhirajlal: The Indian Penal Code, 34th edition"[vii], the author, while discussing the essentials to be satisfied to avail the insanity defense as entailed under Section 84 of the IPC, states that this provision of the statute must be read along with Section 105 of the Indian Evidence Act, 1872. While this is done, the provision of the Evidence Act places the burden of proof on the defendant/ accused and it is pointed out that there is no conflict between the burden that rests on the prosecution to prove the case and the special burden that rests with the accused to avail the insanity defence. Further, the author gives detailed case analyses and comments on the defence through the chapter on Section 84 of the IPC in the book.

In the book "K.D. Gaur: Textbook on Indian Penal Code 7th edition"[viii], the author introduces an interesting fact that Idaho, a state in the U.S. which is known to have created a good number of insanity defence tests itself, does not allow insanity as a defence to criminal charges. However, this restriction can allow expert medical opinion to provide a persuasive opinion on the mental state of the accused and how it must have been during the commission of the act. This indicates that the state allows conviction of possibly insane people who have the ability to analyse the rightness and wrongness of the act they commit.

Suresh Bada Math and two other authors in their journal article titled 'Insanity Defense: Past, Present and Future[ix]' explores the defence in a detailed manner. What attracts the reader's attention is how the authors have elaborated upon the quintessential role that a psychiatrist can play in judging the mental condition of the accused. Since legal insanity and medical insanity differ from each other, the Courts till date haven't placed advanced/ expert medical opinion in a stature of importance to determine insanity but a standard/ uniform procedure to decide upon the insanity of the persons who plead it via Section 84 of the IPC is very much required. Psychiatrists, who now deal with treatment of convicts (who were punished under the premise of Guilty but Mentally Ill) can be asked to certify mental illnesses of the accused and certify whether the person is mentally and emotionally balanced to go through the procedures of the Court to establish his innocence and avail the defence of insanity.

<u>HISTORY AND ORIGIN OF THE DEFENCE</u>

The first-ever case regarding the defence of insanity dates back to 1724. It was an English law judgment (R. v. Arnold[x]) which put forward the Wild Beast Test. The Wild Beast Test for insanity followed the logic that a person will be immune from liability for the act that was committed by him/ her on the premise that he/ she was not aware of the nature of the act or whether the act done was right or wrong.

Later, the Hadfield case of 1800 introduced the Insane Delusion Test which states that the person must have been in an insane delusion (false belief or apprehension that will not be perceived by a rational person) and that the said delusion must have to be proved as the reason for the commission of the crime.

After this came the Bowler's case of 1812 which established a test in which the Court would have to determine whether the accused possessed the ability to determine whether his/ her act was right or wrong. This test, however, did not serve as a clear-cut indicator of liability.

The case of R. v. M'Naghten in 1843 explored the insanity defence in a detailed manner and entailed that the defence requires two elements:

- Presence of mental defect (which can be a defect of reason or a disease of the mind).
- Mental defect must have caused a cognitive impairment to the accused by which he/ she does not know the nature and calibre of the act done by him/ her.

The case also laid down rules for the application of the defence of insanity:

- Generally, it is presumed that every man is sane and is aware of what he is doing and the responsibility that he holds for each of his acts, until proved otherwise.
- If the accused was aware of what he was doing or had only a partial insane delusion, then he/ she will be held liable for the criminal act committed.
- It must be clearly established that the accused had operated with an unsound mind.
- To avail the defence of insanity, it must be proved that, at the time of the act, the accused was not aware/ did not have the capacity to be aware of the nature and consequences of his/ her act. He/ She did not know whether the act was right or wrong.

These rules laid down in the M'Naghten case constitute the 'Right and Wrong Test' which is the most important, accurate and widely followed test with respect to the application of the defence of insanity. This test, along with the case, happened to be the base for the formulation of Section 84 of the IPC.

ESSENTIALS TO BE SATISFIED TO USE THE INSANITY DEFENCE

Three important essentials (entailed by the author in the introduction of the paper) have to be satisfied in the case for the accused to be able to exempt himself from liability/ responsibility using the insanity defence.

Out of the three essentials, the first one is that the unsound mind of the accused during the commission of the act must be established. To establish this, it is necessary that the insanity adheres with the definition of legal insanity and not mere medical insanity.

Difference between medical insanity and legal insanity

Insanity, as indicated under Section 84 of the IPC, means the lack or absence of maturity/ clear understanding of the act done and the ill state of mind (unsoundness). When it comes to unsoundness of the mind, the definition differs from the medical and legal points of view. Simply, it can be told that any person committing a crime is insane and so, can avail the insanity defence but not every form of mad, crazy or insane behaviour/ act acknowledged by law shall ensure exemption from criminal liability. This view was affirmed by the Apex Court when it said that "Every mentally ill person is not ipso facto exempt from criminal responsibility.

A distinction needs to be made between legal insanity and medical insanity."[xi] The Supreme Court further held that legal insanity holds importance in a court of law while deciding liability and not medical insanity. For example: Partial insane delusion, sudden provocation to do a rash act, psychopathic behaviour etc do not attract exemption from criminal liability on the grounds of insanity as they do not constitute as incapacity of the person to be aware of the nature, rightness or wrongness of the act.

Predominantly, insanity is considered as a mental aspect. Even if a person is mentally/ medically insane, it is not necessary that he is legally insane too. Medical insanity can be mental illnesses like Alzheimer, psychotic behaviour, inability of the person to distinguish between fictionality and reality, mental deficiency that occurs due to age, accidents or injuries, low IQ (Intelligence Quotient) and other conditions similar to this. Conditions of medical insanity has the persons under medication but they have the capacity to make decisions of their own and be aware of the consequences of their act. Medical insanity takes into account the past behaviour and acts of the person.

Legal insanity, on the other hand, can consist of a combination of the any of the conditions mentioned above with the incapacity of the person to be aware of the nature, rightness or wrongness of the act. Legal insanity can be better described as a mental illness/ unsound state coupled with the absence of reasoning power. This condition must exist during the commission of the act, which in turn exempts the person from liability for the criminal act committed as it was committed by him/ her without knowledge of its nature and consequences.

The unsoundness of mind of the person immediately preceding and succeeding the act done will be a relevant fact to exempt liability.[xii] Furthermore, the opinion of a medical expert regarding the mental state and behaviour of the accused will not hold utmost or final binding on the Courts. Their opinion would be of a persuasive nature and the Judges will have to decide on the applicability of the defence of insanity with respect to the proof established by the accused himself and the facts pertaining to the particular case. In simpler words, "It is the totality of the circumstances seen in the light of the recorded evidence that would prove whether the offence was committed."[xiii]

Incapable of knowing the nature of the act committed

The second essential to be satisfied is that the person must be incapable of knowing/ not aware of the nature of the act while committing it. To satisfy this essential, the accused must have been entirely oblivious to what he/ she was doing and the effects and repercussions of the same. This state of being of the accused would also mean that the accused is legally insane and he lacks the ability to judge the outcomes, quality, criminal nature of his/ her act.

It is not enough if the aforementioned aspects had just occurred but it must be successfully established by the accused in the court of law in order for him/ her to avail the defence.

Incapable of knowing whether the act was right or wrong or contrary to the provisions of law

To avail the insanity defence, the accused must prove that he/ she committed the act when he/ she was not aware whether it is right or wrong or contrary to law. For this essential to be satisfied, the accused need not be entirely insane. Even if the accused is informed/ well aware of the nature and consequences of his/ her act, a proof of his/ her inability to have the knowledge of whether the act committed is right or wrong is enough to apply the defence provision. By the word wrong, it can mean either legally wrong or both legally and morally wrong.

No matter whether the standard for consideration is either of the two mentioned above, if there surfaces any evidence or proof that indicates the attempt to hide, cover-up or conceal material items or facts that might help in establishing criminal liability, it automatically gives out the conclusion that the accused was aware of right and wrong and goes on to nullify M'Naughten's rule.

Usage of the defence of insanity and related provisions/ concepts

The defence of insanity is usually pleaded in felony cases i.e., cases involving crimes with a higher degree of seriousness like murder, manslaughter, kidnapping, burglary etc. What comes across as a related concept to this defence is the concept of diminished responsibility.

DIMINISHED RESPONSIBILITY

The theory of diminished responsibility is a defence, which, if established, will hold the accused liable for culpable homicide/ manslaughter and not murder. This concept/ doctrine has been entailed in Section 2 of the Homicide Act of 1957. This statutory provision states that in a case where a person is found to have killed someone, he will be liable for a decreased degree of crime i.e., manslaughter and not murder if it is proved that the person suffered some mental defect whose influence caused him to do the criminal act, without him actually knowing the nature and effects of the act.

GUILTY BUT MENTALLY ILL

In relation to insanity, this is a verdict that is now frequently passed by the courts of law. In these kinds of cases, the person with a mental defect who committed the criminal act is not eligible to avail the defence of insanity as his condition does not match with the essentials to avail the defence. He is punished and in addition, given treatment for his mental condition while serving his term of imprisonment.

LANDMARK INDIAN CASE LAWS

Ratan Lal v. State of Madhya Pradesh[xiv]

In this case, the appellant set ablaze the grass in a piece of land. He reasoned his act by saying that he burnt it and the onlookers could do whatever they wished. He was charged with Section 435 of the IPC which gives out punishment for persons causing mischief by fire coupled with an intent to sabotage the area. A psychiatrist was consulted and the expert confirmed that the appellant was a lunatic under the Indian Lunacy Act, 1912 and the report provided by the psychiatrist indicated that the appellant suffered from lunatic depression and needs therapy for the same. On these grounds, the trial court acquitted the appellant. The High Court, on the other hand, overruled the decision of the trial court and made the person liable for his act. The Supreme Court, on an appeal, analysed the case and ruled that the accused could take the defence of insanity under Section 84 of the IPC and acquitted the person. The reasons stated for the acquittal were the medical proof provided and the mental condition of the person at the time of committing the act. These established that the person was insane and was carrying out the act of mischief in an unsound state of mind (without reasoning or knowing the nature of his act).

Shrikant Anandrao Bhosale v. State of Maharashtra[xv]

In this case, a police constable hit his wife on the head with a stone, which in turn caused her death. The police constable was booked for murder. He pleaded the defence of insanity and produced before the Court, evidence of a historical mental illness in his family. The cause of this illness was not known and it was also brought to attention that the constable was under treatment for the same. He lacked motive to kill and no attempt was made by him to conceal or cover-up the criminal act.

Therefore, the Court declared that the constable was mentally defect and showcased incapacity to realise the nature of the act committed by him. The constable was freed from charges by successfully availing the defence of insanity under Section 84 of the IPC.

Sheralli Wali Mohammed v. State of Maharashtra[xvi]

In this case, the offender killed his wife and daughter using a chopper. He was booked for murder. There was a lack of motive on behalf of the offender and he did not make any attempt to flee or hide his act. When he pleaded the defence of insanity, the Court rejected the plea stating that mere lack of motive and absence of attempt to conceal facts is not enough to attract the defence of insanity. The defence can help in the exemption of liability only for those persons who have a mental defect and by reason of such defect are unable to comprehend the nature, consequences, rightness or wrongness of the act being committed by them.

<u>LAW IN THE UK AND THE USA ON THE DEFENCE OF INSANITY IN COMPARISON WITH THE INDIAN LAW</u>

INSANITY DEFENCE- BRITISH AND INDIAN LAWS

English law, which provided the base for the emergence of Section 84 of the IPC, contains the defence of insanity as a valid defence in criminal law. M'Naughten's rules from the English law judgment of R. v. M'Naghten form the foundation of the insanity defence. Before M'Naghten's case, English Law had experimented with the defence of insanity through the Wild Beast Test and the Insane Delusion Test (explained under Chapter II of this paper), but M'Naughten's rules have been considered as the most accurate and important ones with regards to the usage of the defence. As has been explained earlier from the Indian point of view, in the English circumstances too, the accused, in order to avail the defence of insanity must establish his unsound state of mind during the commission of the act which led to him being unaware or unable to decipher the nature, after-effects or the rightness or wrongness of the act being committed by him.

Irresistible Impulse

Irresistible impulse can be defined as a sudden provocation that incites a person to commit an offence. In Indian Law, irresistible impulse is not considered as a part of the defence of insanity. It does not adhere to the provisions of Section 84 of the IPC as well.

The Apex Court declared that losing self-control or an irrepressible inclination is not a defence under Indian law.[xvii] The Supreme Court, in another instance, adjudged that in a case where a murder is committed on the premise of an irresistible impulse and there being no motive to explain the murder, the defence of insanity cannot be availed[xviii] as there is no indicator hinting at incapacity of the accused to distinguish between right and wrong.

But, under English Law, certain instances with a combination of irresistible impulse and a mental defect and absence of reasoning power can come under the ambit of insanity, thereby attracting the defence under criminal law.

INSANITY DEFENCE- AMERICAN AND INDIAN LAWS

Similar to the Indian circumstances, law in America also had M'Naughten's rules as the forerunner to determine liability in cases where the defence of insanity is pleaded. In addition to this, American Law had the Irresistible Impulse test that was established in 1884. Unlike India, in America, irresistible impulse when coupled with unsoundness of mind in certain circumstances can exempt the doer of the act from liability under the pretext of insanity defence. This view was upheld in the landmark case of Lorena Bobbit[xix]in 1993.

Durham Rule

Later, The United States started making use of the 'Durham Rule' or the 'Product Test' which was introduced in the case of Durham v. United States. The essentials of the Durham Rule are as follows:

- Mental disease or weakness
- Causation of crime through the mental disease

Initially, this case declared the existing tests of Right and Wrong Test (M'Naughten's Rules) and the Irresistible Impulse Test as no longer useful.

Later, it was realised that the existing tests can be used along with the new Durham Rule. Presently, the Durham Rule is followed only in New Hampshire because it is considered to have too broad a scope by other jurisdictions.

Substantial Capacity Test

USA has another test for the insanity defence which is termed as the Substantial Capacity Test. This test was propounded by the Model Penal Code created and published by the American Legal Institute in 1962. This Code assists the existing legislations in the U.S. in the field of criminal law. According to this test, the person committing the act must have a mental defect/ disease and that mental condition must facilitate a volitional act. In order to be exempted from criminal liability, the conclusion of this test must be that the person with the mental defect lacked a substantial capacity to recognise the criminal nature of the act done or adhere with the provisions of law.

CONCLUSION

The author, through this research paper, has studied and presented the defence of insanity in a criminal law viewpoint. How the defence originated, various tests for exemption of criminal liability, their usage presently, comparison of the Indian pointers with the UK and the US, similar concepts to the insanity defence and many more have been discussed in this paper. The modern era guarantees the misuse of the insanity defence to easily exempt liability when the accused actually happens to be aware of the consequences of his/ her act. To avoid misuse of the defence and to follow a standard procedure, Courts can approach the field of forensic psychiatry for aid. Experts from this field will be able to judge the medical (mental) condition of the accused and will also be able to differentiate between legal and medical insanity and help the Courts in the process of justice.

CHAPTER FOUR

INTELLECTUAL PROPERTY AND HEALTH CARE

Author: Kanimozhi T, II year of LL.M.(Intellectual Property Law) from RGSOIPL, IIT Kharagpur

With a colossal explosion of new technological advancements comes the sanguine effects as well as gloom-ridden repercussions on mental health. Technology today has become a pivotal part of everyone's lives regardless of the job that one does and any sort of dependency on technology ends up impacting the mental health unsympathetically. Inventions have adumbrated a burgeoning stir on the road to customised well-being.

Assiduous lives as well as the escalating clever blending of phones, smartwatches, and others have effectuated expanded customised health tracking.

This market appears to be up to the minute and full-grown for patenting such as apps which exclusively pass on details and figures, input assemblage and presentation, and home commodities that are smart themselves possess all smashed rationale in the world of patenting. Intellectual property rights carry their own significance in the health care domain. The analysis of up-to-the-minute treatments and the progress of medicines to achieve medical exigencies necessitates the preservation of ideas as well as innovations.

Patenting has become a gigantic figure in the arenas of biotechnology and medical research, but in the business model of most businesses in linkage with health care, other Intellectual Property areas have turned out to be condemnatory.Any sort of information that is off the record, be it a manufacturing process or any sort of thing that interests a business by staying undisclosed, is very valuable in the health care sector because it plays a considerable role in furthering research. This is where intellectual property comes into the picture, because innovation would assuredly fall remarkably in the non-appearance of a patenting system.Studies portray a linkage with regard to the upsurge of digital technology in our day-to-day lives and a downturn in psychological wellbeing.

Substantial wrangling has been going on in recent times with regard to the issue of safeguarding intellectual property, to a large extent corresponding to making generic medicines accessible. This appears to be peculiarly applicable in domains where drug development is a necessity for the treatment of disease contagion in the region but where the market is not colossal enough to brace the outlays of research. Any sort of upsurge in social media usage could pave the way to seclusion as well as low self-esteem. Furthermore, compulsively keeping tabs on physiological data can bring about health consternation, other eating derangements,body dysmorphia, and finally, not to mention that many health apps are precariously unmonitored.The healthcare system today has advanced because of technological furtherance. Be it big data or genetic engineering, they all have some dependency on inventions that are up to the minute and novel. The amount of research shows how intellectual property is a substantial player in the healthcare sector.

Intangible rights that play a focal role in safeguarding the products of human intellect and modelling are more often than not known as "intellectual property." In today's health care industry, trademarks play a considerable role because brands rely heavily on fame for assistance, occurrence, and immense attribute. The fame of the seller comes into question when a lab or a hospital strives to choose an up-to-the-minute drug for usage or a piece of disinfection apparatus to buy. By virtue of the congenital process that trade secrets and copyrights carry within themselves, they are seen to be barely ubiquitous in the health care industry. Despite the fact that trade secrets are habitually tenacious about bringing something to bear, they appear to be a bit more customary in comparison with copyrights.Another noteworthy facet of intellectual property that applies in the health care sector is design patents. The inoperable and artistic attributes of a product, for example, the ocular design or its fineness, are what design patents endeavour to safeguard. This becomes so germane in the context that these amiable design facets could, in some ways, pave the way for alleviating stress as clinics and hospitals are more often than not places of pressure for patients and their families.

With a clear understanding of intellectual property and its relation to the health care sector, what should be analysed is whether or not the intellectual property profession is cultivating optimistic attitudes in the workplace. Adjustable working hours become a valuable concern for Intellectual property professionals . Nevertheless, mental well-being is not circumscribed to the Intellectual Property sector; any working professional, by nature, has a need to feel comfortable in their role in order to come up with preferable work.Intellectual property professionals should not be discouragedfrom blatantly holding discussions on details that ought to have consequential destructive effects on them in their corresponding parts. It is advantageous to express these issues blatantly or any kind of lifestyle requirements to the client early on, as this may be a more optimistic stratagem than endeavouring to make eleventh-hour alterations. Adjustable working hours and mental well-being are exceedingly linked, so the same has to be brought into discussion while contemplating a posting.

The genuine triumph of intellectual property systems is exceedingly dependent on their potential to control human behaviour in relation to inventiveness and creativity. Furthermore, accelerating innovatory activity, human behaviour is also a condemnatory facet of intellectual property rights. Acquiescence is a topic that is at present at the midpoint of indubitable international relations and trade disputes. Intellectual property law has a substantial impact on human behaviour, controlling both inventors and users. For all of the above-mentioned reasons, human conduct and psychology play a stupendous role in how intellectual property systems operate in the honest-to-goodness world. Consequently, the mental make-up of intellectual property rights could be perceived as remaining at a curvature point in the middle of an upstream sequence of analytic and inspirational antecedents and the downstream discernible activities that intellectual property law is on the lookout for encouragement.There are a lot of input constituents, such as social, legal, cultural, and economic impacts, that model an individual's fathoming of intellectual property rights.

Furthermore, this psychological grasp of intellectual property rights navigates discernible pursuit in the matter of discrete determinations as well as conclusions in enthralling in productive endeavours and putting money on resources in invention. Fathoming the psychological aspects of intellectual property, its impacts, delineations, and repercussions will strengthen our perception of intellectual property rights and facilitate our ability to better model intellectual property law to pull off preferred aftereffects. Intellectual property supports the funding of research and development, and that is why it is a significant pillar of our health system. Intellectual property will proceed to disentangle curatives for prevailing overdue exigencies as it has upgraded research levels in the health sector.

CHAPTER FIVE

MARITAL RAPE: IS SPOUSAL EXCEPTION VALID?

Author: Priyanshi Bajaj, pursuing B.B.A.,LL.B. from O.P.Jindal Global University

'Rape' is defined under section 375 of the Indian Penal Code,1860 where an essential ingredient to recognize the crime is lack of consent. This section mentions an exception for married couples who can be a victim for the same offense.

<u>**"Exception 2 —Sexual intercourse by a man with his own wife, the wife not being under fifteen years of age, is not rape."**</u>

'Marital rape' is an offense which is committed where the perpetrator is the husband of the victim. Only 52 countries have recognized marital rape as a crime. In India, the reason behindnot criminalizing marital rape and including this exception is discussed by the law commissions, parliamentary debates and even inthe judicial decisions. The reasons advanced by such organizations are broadly to protect the sanctity of the institution of marriage and mentioning of existing alternative remedies for women in the law.

Four primary justifications were proposed for not criminalizing marital rape in India. The reasons put forth were a clear manifestation of the interplay between marital rape and protecting marriage from the interference of law.

First and foremost, argument, that was put forth was based out of a preconceived notion that women were subdued by their husband. The premise on which marital rape was not criminalized was essentially based on the idea that women did not have any rights in the marriage and belonged to the husbands. The husband was the master of the wife and enjoyed complete rights over her body. Women being a chattel to their husband was not allowed to revolt against anything. The same ideology was adopted back then for framing laws for adultery.

The second justification for not identifying marital rape as a crime was because of the theory of unities. This theory states that after marriage, the identity of a women is merged with that of her husband and they do not have any individual recognition. Women are associated with the man and they do not have any individual voice to frame any opinion.

The next justification given after a feminist revolutionafter 1970 was based on the rationale of implied consent theory. Here, an incontestable presumption of consent is taken into consideration when two people are bound by the civil contract of marriage. Participation in sexual activities is thought to be defining an important element of the civil contract. When two people enter into this contract of marriage, it is deduced that those people have allowed themselves to engage in sexual activities during all point of time in the unification.

The fourth argument raised in the recent times for not validating marital rape as a sin is because it is thought that criminal law must not interfere between the marital relationships between husband and wife. It is considered to be a matter within the private sphere of those individuals where law must not be allowed to penetrate. It is further substantiated by saying that if law intervenes in such private matters it would be doing a greater injustice in the society than protecting women from such cruelty.

The consent for sexual activities had been interpreted differently by the courts in different instance. For example, an interpretation of section 376B of the Indian Penal Code,1860 would clearly manifest that living together raises a presupposition of consent to sexual intercourse by the husband. The law holds charges against a husband if he forcefully asks his wife to engage in sexual activities with him if they are living separately during that time. It is not reasonable for the courts to shield the crime of rape from the operation of law if two people are living together.

In 2012, the Criminal law amendment bill replaced the word 'rape' with 'sexual assault' in order to widen the scope of the crime but still it did not accommodate any provision to criminalize marital rape. The suggestions proposed by the J.S. Verma report were not even taken into consideration. The standing committee formed during that time rejected the recommendation of striking off the exception clause of section 375 of the Indian Penal Code on broadly two grounds. Essentially it said that if law is allowed to perforate into the matters of the 'private sphere' of a family, the whole family system would be under stress and the courts would be doing more injustice to the whole network prevalent in the society. The next argument was that sufficient remedies already existed for a woman to take a legal recourse in case she is being subjected to domestic violence or cruelty by her family. The remedy in criminal law is through the concept of cruelty as mentioned in section 498A of the Indian Penal Code,1860. They can also seek recourse through the Protection of women from domestic violence Act, 2005. The essence of the reasoning is that criminalization of marital rape does not fit into the Indian context because of the established idea of the society to treat marriage as sacrament. This question has been avoided by the legislation by saying that the matter has been taken up but still no decisions were given. The judiciary has disregarded petitions to strike down the exception clause. The goal is to protect the conjugal rights of individuals.

The culture has played an important role in shaping the law of the country. The state's selective intervention with the private sphere even when the women is undergoing cruelty is problematic. The step taken back by the state to provide legal justice when a married woman is being raped by her own husband is degrading to human dignity and monstrous to human spirit.

In the case of Independent thought v. Union of India 2018, it was decided by the court to strike down a part of the exception clause of section 375 of the Indian Penal Code,1860. Under Protection of children from sexual offences Act, 2012 (POCSO) it is illegal to have sexual intercourse with a child under eighteen years of age but the exception clause mentioned in the Indian Penal Code,1860 allows a man for this affair if the girl that he is married to is between the age of fifteen and eighteen. This differential treatment by the state exclusively on the basis of marriage is unreasonable and unconstitutional.

Rape should also be treated differently from grievous hurt or assault. It has a different threshold in the evidence law as well. Rape is associated with complex patriarchal and power structures of the society. Therefore, there is a stark difference between the nature and act of rape from the act of cruelty on women. The law must allow specific criminalization of marital rape to note that the rapist or the perpetrator has violated the law and not only the body of the victim. The offense of cruelty is a ground for divorce but does not accommodate sexual offenses committed on a married woman. Therefore, the argument that in case a woman needs a legal help when she is abused sexually it can seek recourse through section 498A of the Indian Penal code,1860 should not be validated.

The next argument raised that criminalization of rape would be too much interference with the family system as it can be dealt within the family itself and a crime should not be criminalized because it is culturally acceptable by the majority of the society should also not be affirmed. Laws and regulations regarding ill practices like sati, dowry and special privileges provided to the lower caste and minority are instances where these practices were widely acceptable by the majority of the society but still reforms were needed to identify whether an act was wrong or not.

If marital rape is not taken up as a specific crime and is allowed in the country then there is a clear violation of Article 14 of the constitution of India which provides women equal rights and autonomy over her body as much as a man enjoys.

Four prong suggestion to effectively criminalize rape by J.S. Verma report must be regarded and there should be no reason to validate spousal exception in cases of rape. Hence, accused in marital rape must be charged with same sentencing policies as adopted in commitment of crime like rape.

CHAPTER SIX

CRITICAL ANALYSIS OF SECTION 29A OF INSOLVENCY AND BANKRUPTCY CODE 2016

Author: Lakshay Mehta, V year of B.A.,LL.B. from Ideal School of Law, Ip university

What is Insolvency and Bankruptcy Code?

The Insolvency and Bankruptcy Code 2016, provides for the time bound process to resolve the insolvency. Whenever there is a default in the reimbursement, then the creditors gain control over the corporate debtor's assets and needs to take the decision required to solve the insolvency. So, the resolution process may be initiated by either creditor or debtor. This code is such an effective mechanism for the lenders, suppliers and different creditors to ensure payment of the loan.

What was the objective behind Insolvency and Bankruptcy Code?

The sole objective behind implementing Insolvency and Bankruptcy Code 2016 was that to provide the balance between the stakeholders of company i.e. they can enjoy availability of credit and such loss which creditor needs to bear on the account of the default. The basic reason behind implementing the Insolvency and Bankruptcy Code was that to establish the Insolvency and Bankruptcy Board of India as the regulative body for the Insolvency and Bankruptcy Law.

What is Section 29 A?

The Section 29 A of the Insolvency and Bankruptcy Code 2016 was introduced through the Insolvency and Bankruptcy Amendment Act 2017. It essentially restricts certain person for submitting the resolution plan throughout the corporate insolvency process. It restricts the wilful defaulter, undischarged insolvent or the promoter of the company among others are then restricted from becoming resolution applicant and prohibits them from submitting the resolution plan.

Reason behind implementation of Section 29 A

The main reason behind the introduction of Section 29A in the Insolvency and Bankruptcy Amendment Act 2017 is that there was nothing being mandated by the law which might prohibit the ineligible person under to make an application under the Section 230 of the Act. So, before the Section 29 A, every individual or the body corporate will participate in the bidding process of the corporate debtor that is being subjected to the Corporate Insolvency Resolution Process irrespective of whether or not he's the initial promotor, director or the person that is connected to them either directly or indirectly. This basic loophole within the Insolvency and Bankruptcy Code 2016 helps the person who by their misconduct or the deceitful motive that directly results in the default of the corporate debtor and the person can again regain the control of the Corporate Debtors by basically bidding in the significant discounts, while making the banks suffering so much losses/haircuts.

Applicability of Section 29 A

The application needs to be filed by the resolution applicant before the National Company Law Tribunal by seeking the permission to grant the approval of the resolution plan and to held that he's not being disbarred or he is not being disqualified under the provisions of the Section 29 A of the Insolvency and Bankruptcy Code 2016. So, the Section 29 is basically applicable to all whether the person is a sole resolution applicant or jointly with the other persons and he is not violating any provisions in regard to the Section 29 A.

What is Resolution Plan?

Under the Section 5(26) of the Insolvency and Bankruptcy Code 2016 it is a plan which is being proposed by any person. For the Insolvency Resolution of the corporate debtor it must be going concern which is in accordance with the Part II.

What is resolution applicant?

The Resolution Applicant means a person who individually or being jointly with any person, submits the resolution plan to the resolution professional which is pursuant to the invitations made under the clause (h) of the sub section (2) of the Section 25.

Who is ineligible to be resolution applicant?

According to the Section 29 A of Insolvency and Bankruptcy Code,2016 the following persons are basically ineligible to be resolution applicant:

A. A person is found to be undischarged insolvent i.e. he is unable to repay his debts and as long as he is unable to repay debts, he is an undischarged insolvent.

B. A person is a wilful defaulter i.e. despite having sufficient means to make payment of his pending dues still he refuses to comply with demand made by guarantor.

C. He is basically convicted for the offence which is punishable and liable for imprisonment for 2 years or more.

Also, the person who has been disqualified to act as the director under the Company Act 2013 or is prohibited by the SEBI for accessing the security market, are ineligible to become resolution applicant.

Four Layers for the Ineligibility under Section 29 A of IBC

1. The person himself is found to be ineligible.
2. The person connected to the ineligible person is also ineligible.
3. The person related to the ineligible person is also ineligible.
4. The person acting jointly or in concern with the ineligible person.

(As per the Section 240 A of the Insolvency and Bankruptcy Code 2016, the provisions of the clauses (c) and (h) will not be applicable to the resolution applicant with respect to the corporate insolvency process of the micro, medium and any small enterprises.)

Case Laws

1. RBL Bank Limited vs MBL Infrastructures[i]: In this case while interpreting the clause (h) of the Section 29 A of the Insolvency and Bankruptcy Code 2016 saying that the object of the clause (h) of the Section 29 is not to disqualify the promoters as the class for submitting the resolution plan. The basic reasoning behind insertingthe clause (h) was to exclude such guarantors from offering of their resolution plan on the account of their antecedent which may adversely affect the resolution process. Thus, the National Company Law Tribunal held that one has to consider that whether guarantee has been invoked or the guarantor has made any default. If none of the elements which were discussed above then there will be no case for the disqualifications for the defaulter,

2. JaypeeInfratechv/s Axis Bank Limited[ii]: This case has clarified the questions regarding the application and the scope of the section 29 A of the Insolvency and Bankruptcy Code 2016. In this case while dealing with the eligibility of the Jai Prakash Associates Limited, the parent company of the Jaypee Infratech Limited as the resolution application under the Section 29A Insolvency and Bankruptcy Code. The Supreme Court held that the Jai Prakash Associates have been disqualified from submitting the resolution plan as they fall within scope of section 29 A thus, they are ineligible. Therefore, the strict adherence to the Section 29 A is mandatory so the wilful defaulters shall not be permitted to participate in the corporate insolvency resolution process.

3. Standard Chartered Bank DBS Bank Ltd Vs Ruchi Soya Industries Ltd[iii]-: In this committee of the creditors (COC) has declared the Adani Wilmar has the highest bidder therefore the resolution plan has been finalized. After being dissatisfied by the decision of the Committee of the Creditors, so the claim of the ineligibility under the Section 29 A of the Insolvency and Bankruptcy Code 2016 has been raised by the Patanjali Ayurveda (second bidder). Therefore, in this case the Adani Wilmer is claimed to be ineligible because spouse of the managing director of the Adani Wilmer is the daughter of the defaulting promotor. Thus, Patanjali Ayurveda has approached the National Company Law Tribunal challenging the decision of the committee of the creditors for appointing the Adani

Wilmar.

<u>Conclusion</u>

The Section 29 A has laid down the multiple layers and comprehensive standard of the disqualification that will also exclude the bona fide resolution applicants. This section might also disbar the crucial shareholders trying to bid for revival of the company. Thus, there must be certain amount of the leniency to be provided by the courts in deciding the disqualification to maximise the objectives of the Insolvency and Bankruptcy Code.

As prior to the inclusion of the Section 29 A there was no bar on the eligibility of the resolution applicant so any person can become the resolution applicant. So, this led to the open-ended platform for the defaulters to bid for the assets undergoing the corporate insolvency process by taking undue advantage of this provision which would defeat the vary purpose of the Insolvency and Bankruptcy Code,2016. Thus, in order to curtail the same, the Section 29 A was introduced, so Section 29 A not only restricts the promoters but also the people who are related to the promoter. The basic reasoning behind the introduction of the Section 29 was to restrict those persons from submitting the resolution plan which could cause the adverse effect on the entire corporate insolvency process

STALKING LAWS AND OUTCOME OF INDIAN MOVIES

Author: Pooja Yadav, pursuing B.B.A LL.B (Hons.) from Narsee Monjee Institute Of Management and Science, School of Law, Indore Campus.

WORKING HYPOTHESIS

- Stalking is a criminal offence under Indian Penal Code.
- Stalking causes mental or physical harm to the victims.
- Victims of Stalking commits Suicide because of fear, pressure and threat.
- Any working women, housewives, school girl and college student can be the victim of stalking.
- Sometime men are also the victim of stalking.
- Indian movies portraying and promoting stalking directly or indirectly.

ABSTRACT

In India Stalking was added in criminal law after 2013 Criminal Amendment Act which was passed by Justice Verma Committee. Stalking was added in criminal law because of increase in number of crimes against modesty of women in society. Stalking is not a gender biased crime but in India most commonly stalking is held against women. In India anyone can be stalked at anytime. Before the amendment the term stalking was not directly included in the Penal Code of India. It was just included under harassment like voyeurism and sexual harassment against women, under section 354 and 509. Because of increasing number of cases, it became very necessary to make a separate law for stalking. Before the amendment it was very difficult to punish the offender. And they are moving freely from the court without any fear.

Due to stalking many of the girls commits suicide, suffers mental pressure or some suffers physical harassment. Some stalkers are so obsessive and after listening no from girl they start torturing them. Torture may be physical or mental. Stalking is often a precursor to other more violent crime.[1] Other more violent crimes like murder, rape, sexual harassment, acid attack etc.

Indian movies play a big role to promote stalking. They were portraying stalking as a cool act. They are showing that stalking is not a crime. They are showing that by following a girl, singing song for a girl, sending present to a girl and protecting a girl from stranger will somehow attract the girls attention towards them. Not all the viewers but some of them are thinking that yes what is all shown in the movie is good and cool and they start doing that all in their real life. But in realty the stalkers open the door of jail for them by doing all that. Stalking is most commonly done by young and teenager peoples. Indian movies are somewhere providing the idea to the people how to stalk anyone. I is not like that movies are only influencing bad things. Movies are not only teaching the bad things to the people I think somewhere it is depending on the peoples mentality, what they are thinking and taking from the movie.

KEY WORDS: Stalking, Victims, Threat, Fear, physical torture, suicide, mental pressure, harassment, obsessive, nonconsensual communication, follow, implied threat, Indian Movie, Indian Penal Code, Stalkers.

INTRODUCTION

Stalking is a criminal offence defined under Indian Penal Code.[2] It is defined by statutes and by court decisions interpreting those statutes.[3] Stalking puts a mental pressure or threat on the victims. The danger and terror a victim of stalking feels has no way to resolve it. In most of the reported cases there is inclusion of male stalkers and female victims. Stalking is an important policy issue for the criminal justice system, for advocates concerned about violence against women and for agencies providing services to victims of crime.[4] Stalking should not be a gender biased crime. But in our Country Stalking is mainly held against women. Stalking is communication crime[5] like stalker is somehow conveying this message to the victim that he is trying to get her consent and in this way it was communicated. An unwanted and/or repeated watching or following or caring to an another person by an individual or group of people is called stalking. Many of the times someone get stalked even without having knowledge that she / he is getting stalked by someone. In our society until a legal action is not taken against someone, it is not accepted as a crime. Because sometimes peoples are not aware of that crime and not having knowledge that there are some laws regarding that crime.

In 1860 Indian Penal Code became a colonial law. At that time Stalking is not mentioned in Indian Penal Code as an offence. At that time Section 354 and section 509 only provides the protection to women. Section 354 covers the offence related to sexual harassment and section 509 covers the offences related to using words or gestures to insult a woman's modesty. If anyone is assaulting a women believing that it will offend the modesty of women is liable under section 354 to be prosecuted by law. There are three tests which will proof that the act is illegal or not.

1). "The act must be against a women,"

2). "The perpetrator must have used excessive force, and"

3). "Their modesty should be offended."

There are a lot of movies where stalking is shown very often. Indian Movies are portraying stalking as a cool and good act. They are showing that following a girl, commenting on a girl, singing a song for a girl is a romanticizing act and not putting any stress on girls. They are showing that this is a good way to get the consent of a girl and girls do not have any problem from that. Indian Movies are showing stalker as a hero of the film and he is following heroine singing some songs for her and after sometime he will get the consent of girl. Indian Movies are conveying that, stalking does not put any mental pressure or physical injury to girl. But in reality it is not true, many of the victims of stalking are facing mental pressure and physical injury. So many victims are there who are not able to bear that mental pressure and commits suicide. Some commits suicide because of fear of society, family and also because of some threat. The victim of stalking are not only young girls but also the married women, working women and school and college going girls. There are a lot of movies since

19's in which stalking scenes are shown and now also it is in the tradition of Indian Movies to show stalking. Tere Naam, Anjam, Darr, Badrinath Ki Dulhaniya, Toilet Ek Prem Katha and Deewana Mujhsa Nahin etc. These are some movies in which scenes of stalking is shown and also the stalkingful songs are also shown where hero is singing song and following the girl at everywhere knowingly that she is not interested, still he is troubling her and at last of the song or at last of the movie the heroine finally consents the hero. And after watching all these stuff people are thinking that it is true and tries this all thing in their real life and faces a lot of troubles and causing injury to others.

In this research I am just trying to show that how from 19's to till now Indian movies are showing Stalking. In many of the movies, stories are supporting the crime of Stalking and in some of the movies they are showing that how stalking is affecting the victims and in some movies that how Stalking leads to other heinous crimes. Various movies shows that how "stalking leads to a positive outcome."

In 1994 Anjaam movie was released in which Shahrukh Khan was playing the role of a psycho and stalker. The whole movie is filled with stalking, and murder. Shahrukh Khan was named as Vijay Agnihotri and Madhuri Dixit was named as Shivani Chopra. Here Shivani is the victim of stalking. This movie shows that how a girl or a women get affected by their stalkers badly in their life. In this movie Vijay is stalking Shivani but she is not aware that someone is stalking her. In this movie Vijay reaches Shivani's home to sign her as model but she denied. For some meeting Vijay had booked tickets of flight for London but then at airport he saw Shivani, she is going on duty for Air India Dubai, so now to follow Shivani Vijay asked receptionist to change the ticket from London to Dubai and he bored the dubai flight then in the flight he called Shivani and asked to bring a drink for him she said Ok. Immediately he again press the bell and called Shivani she turned and he said that or commented that "drink should have to be more addictive than her eyes and more spicy than her tongue."

When the flight reached Dubai every passenger leaved the flight Vijay also leaved. But after hearing that the same flight is backing for Mumbai Vijay again bored the flight for Shivani. After watching him again Shivani get surprised. In the flight Vijay again irritated Shivani. When flight land on Mumbai Vijay started singing song for Shivani at front of everyone but she ignored and went from there.

This movie shows that how Vijay stalks Shivani after her marriage also. He is following her at every place where she is going with her husband and family. At one point Vijay asked Shivani to marry with him but she denied and shouted on him and said that she is a married women. Then to marry her with a malice intention Vijay murdered Shivani's husband in hospital.

This movie shows that how a stalker from the normal stalking stage comes up to the stage of heinous crimes. How they become obsessive towards anything.

In 2003 movie Tere Naam was released in this movie there are some scenes which are related to stalking here Salman Khan is the hero and acting as a stalker. In this movie Salman Khan is playing the role of Radhe Mohan and Bhumika Chawla is playing the role of simple girl Nirjara. Here in this movie Radhe Mohan Proposes Nirjara to marry after meeting and talking to her 3 to 5 times. Radhe Mohan just make a perception in his mind that she is also loving to him and ready to marry because Nirjara did not replied anything in fear in the college. He also blackmailed Nirjara's pheonsay that he should not move or talk to Nirjara because he is going to marry her. Next day Radhe catches the train and waiting for the Nirjara because he knows that she is travelling from train to reach the college. Nirjara catches the train and she is not knowing that Radhe is following her, waiting for her in the train. She entered the train and find a sit, and she saw at the front of her Radhe was there. In the train Radhe started talking to her like now we are going to marry don't scare with the peoples think about ourself and tried to give present to her and said that it will look beautiful on her feet, after listening all this rubbish she got scared but then she denied because she is not liking that all. She requested that please stop talking to me like this because she is not interested in that all and somewhere all this act is defaming her she is feeling fear of reputation but still Radhe keep on convincing her at last she shouted and went from there. After sometime Radhe again followed her and tried to stop her in the way and tried to talk her and convince her, she again shouted and moved on her way where she is going. Now Radhe kidnapped her this time and started expressing his feelings and tried to convince her Nirjara tried to ran but she did not succeeded. After this all she got scared and cried than Radhe tried to beat her also but he stopped. Radhe said that he wants to keep her happy and he is not a bad person, he will care her like a queen and then after all it is a movie at the last of all these heroine Bhumika Chawla that is Nirjara consented him to marry.

In 2013 Raanjhanaa movie was released in this movie Dhanush is playing the act of stalker named Kundan Shankar and Sonam Kapoor is playing the role of a girl Zoya haider. Kundan is stalking Zoya since her school time. But the movie is showing the situation of stalking look like romance[6] and that's why the people watching this movie also think that following a girl and asking her name again and again is not a crime it's just a little thing. This movie is conveying that Kundan's love is a dedicated love towards Zoya. They are not addressing that how much problematic and real repercussions it has on audiences[7].

Movie shows that how to get the consent and attention of Zoya, Kundan coerces her. He said to her to confess that "she also loves him otherwise he will cut his wrist." Sometime it happens that in reality peoples applying this way to get the consent of a girl, to coerce a girl or in want of doing something filmy and to get the attention of a girl.

In this movie Zoya called him as "jahil" still he keep on following her. The word jahil shows that how much she get irritated or she suffered the nonsense. If any person is in too then he uses this type of words and it also shows that she is nowhere fell in love with him. But it is a trend in our Indian movies that stalking leads to positive outcome[8]. Movie shows that instead of trauma which Zoya faced the story at the end is in the favour of Kundan.

All the above movies shows that how Indian movie are portraying stalking. In first movie stalking leads to murder of victim's husband. In second movie how after getting tortured also victim consented for marriage. In third movie it shows that how to coerce a girl to get her attention and how to force a girl to confess. In Indian society people thinks and it is their mentality that whatever is shown in the television is something good and true because they are only showing what is really happening in the life of peoples or in the world. If we took an example of a child like he is watching his or her favorite cartoon and in that cartoon the lead cartoon is beating an enemy after eating sweats. So the child also thinks that it is true, if I eat beat someone after eating sweats then no one can defeat me. So with this example we can interpret that how a cartoon influences children mind.

In the same way the adults also get influenced after watching the movie some felt that whatever is show in movie was bad and some felt it was good. So here logical thinking is different as compared to child but it is true that peoples get influenced by movies. And it depends on person or on their thinking that what they interpret from the movie. But most probably people thinks the same way what movies are conveying.

A. General Concept of Stalking

In General Stalking is defined as "a course of conduct directed at a specific person that involves repeated visual or physical proximity, nonconsensual communication, or verbal, written, or implied threats, or a combination thereof, that would cause a reasonable person fear."[9] Without the consent of victim, stalker's keep on sending unwanted items and presents and trying to get the consent of victim. They are trying to damage or threaten the victim's property, slander the victim's character, or harassing the victim via the internet by posting personal information or spreading rumors about the victim.[10] It is a type of behavior of stalker's.

Stalking creates a threat and fear in the mind of victims. Threat may be either explicit or implicit. Stalker's commit offence of stalking with the people's whom they know or with whom they have relationship. Stalking can be done either through electronic media or without electronic media. On regular basis many women in India get stalked, she can be a working women, a college student or a housewife.

B. Definition of Stalking under IPC

Stalking is defined under Section 354D of Indian Penal Code

[11]354-D. Stalking - (1) Any man who -

(i) follows a woman and contacts, or attempts to contact such woman to foster personal interaction repeatedly despite a clear indication of disinterest by such woman; or[12]

(ii) monitors the use by a woman of the internet, email or any other form of electronic communication,[13]

commits the offence of stalking[14]

If a person commits the offence of stalking shall be punished with imprisonment and fine. On first conviction criminal shall be punished with imprisonment of either description for a term which may extend to three years and shall also be liable to fine[15]

If a person commits the offence of stalking second time or again he shall be punished with imprisonment of either description for a term which may extend to five years and shall also be liable for fine, further it is provided[16]

C. How Indian Movies are portraying Stalking

Indian Movies are somewhere promoting stalkers to commit the crime of Stalking, because they are showing some scenes or songs where hero is acting as a stalker and trying to get the consent of heroine, knowingly that she is not interested in him but still he is trying, by sending presents, giving flowers, continuously watching her and following her at school, market, till her home etc. And after sometime he get the consent of heroine and that person who is acting as a stalker now became hero and they are enjoying their life. In this way Indian movies are conveying this message to all the audience.

By watching all these stuffs in the cinema our young generation get distracted from the good path. They are thinking that it is cool and girls have no problem with these. If the famous hero is doing that it means it is good and we can do this. It is no crime at all. In this way it Indian movies are hampering the thinking of young generation and not only the young generation other generations too get promoted. Some stalkers who are obsessive and not ready to hear no from girl or women commits heinous crime. Stalkers obviously spoiling their life as well the victim's life.

They are not showing the reality that how stalking puts a mental pressure on a women or girl, how they are feeling threat or under threat, how some girls are facing the physical injury as well by the stalkers. In reality if a girl is not interested in their stalker than it is not possible that by sending presents and romanticizing her stalker will get the consent.

In Indian movies stalking is shown as "cool" and good thing. They are portraying in a way that stalking is not at all crime and due to this a lot of girls are suffering a lot. Some girls are committing suicide in fear of Stalker and lose their precious life.

Following are some movies in which stalking is shown:

1). Badrinath Ki Dulhaniya

2). Toilet : Ek Prem Katha

3). Deewana Mujhsa Nahin

4). Rehna Hai Tere Dil Mein

5). Tere Naam

6). Anjaam

7). Darr

And so many other movies in which stalking scenes are shown. Movies are not directly conveying that we are showing stalking but indirectly this massage is being conveyed to peoples.

D. Impact of Stalking

Impact of stalking on victim is I think depend on victim's mental strongness or weakness may be some victims are mentally so weak and not able to share all the things to anyone or fight for their safety. And may be some victims are mentally so strong, they are able to fight for themselves. Mostly it is severe and psychologically traumatic for many victims who are emotionally weak.[17] There are so many victims who are suffering from mental health disorders and they feel unsafe, pressurized, out of control, and most of the time they may experience a loss of trust, loss of long term emotions from closed ones and it leads to uneasiness, bipolar illness etc.[18] All this habits also result in all time anger and pressure.[19] Sometimes victims change their jobs, change their residence location, change their telephone numbers to protect themselves from stalker. Sometimes victim also carrying weapons or firearms to protect themselves.[20]

In youth and in teenagers the stalking and harassing is mainly usual in India. It is the influence or inspiration from films, series and movies as they are showing that following a girl or boy, making comments and showing love and care or sending presents is a heroic thing.

E. Stalking In India

There was no direct insertion of the term stalking in penal law of India before the amendment in criminal laws. Before the amendment stalking was just covered under the category of harassment such as voyeurism and sexual harassment against women. And it was covered under section 354 and section 509 of Indian Penal Code for using words or gestures to insult a women's modesty.[21] In lots of cases the stalker or criminals moves freely without any fear from the court. It is hard to proof the certain necessary conditions to constitute a crime.[22] Stalkers moves freely because of the imperfections in the essentials of section 354 and section 509 Indian Penal Code.[23] Therefore it was became need to make separate law for stalking in India.

F. Amendment In Stalking

Amendment in Stalking law is done after the Delhi gang rape case i.e. Nirbhaya Case. 16, December 2012 is the day when jyoti sing 23 year old girl physiotherapy intern was raped, tortured and beaten by six men in the bus and her friend was also being beaten by them. After this case most concrete steps was taken by the Indian Government. To curb the violence against women Criminal Law Amendment Act 2013 has been one of the most concrete steps taken by the Indian Government. Criminal Law was amended as well as new sections are also inserted in the Indian Penal Code with regard to various sexual offences.[24] After this amendment a separate section i.e. section 354D is made in Indian Penal Code to cover the Stalking cases. Under section 354 D punishment is also specified by law-makers on first conviction criminal is punished with imprisonment of three years and also liable to fine. If someone is committing the offence of stalking again and again then he shall be punished with imprisonment of five years and also liable to fine.

G. Stalking : A Bailable Offence

In India Stalking is bailable offence when it is committed by someone for the first time.[25] When punishment is given for the first time for three years then accuse may get the bail from the court but if the crime is committed by someone for second time or again and again then accuse will not get the bail from court. Stalking is sometime became a first step for commission of other crimes like rape, murder, acid attack, kidnapping and etc.[26] If court will not allow bail to peoples on the first conviction then may be there is chances that some people will not commit the same crime again because of deterrence. But when the court grant the bail order to the accuse then the accuse move freely on the road and then to take revenge they commit other crimes as well like rape, acid attack and etc.

After the Delhi gang rape i.e. Nirbhaya Case the Justice Verma Committee suggested that to present formally stalking as a non-bailable offence on the first convction as well.[27] The UPA government also agreed with this bill of making, stalking as a non bailable offence for the first time. And the Parliamentary Standing Committee also agreed. But then because of some opposite parties argument and opposition the bill was not passed and stalking remain bailable offence on first conviction. "This is a massive Lacuna in stalking law."[28]

CONCLUSION

Stalking means following someone, watching someone, sending presents, and singing songs and commenting on someone knowingly that he/she is not interested. Stalking can be done by both boy and girl. But in our country stalking is mainly done against women. Any women can be stalked at any time, she can be a school going girl, college girl, working women or any housewife. Stalking is a communicated crime. At previous time stalking is not properly defined in any of the laws. It is only covered under section 354 and 509. Section 354 covers offences related to sexual harassment and section 509 covers offences related to using words or gestures to insult a women's modesty.

There is no any specific section available in Indian Penal Code which covers the crime related to stalking. After the Nirbhaya gang rape case government has taken a very concrete step to amend the criminal law.

In India after the Criminal Amendment Act 2013 stalking was separately defined under section 354 D. The Criminal Amendment Act 2013 was passed by the Justice Verma Committee to stop the increasing cases of stalking and to secure the girl child and women of the country from stalking.

In India peoples are not considering anything as crime until the legislature make strict laws for that. There are so many victims who are not aware that how to file complaint for the crime like stalking. Common peoples are not knowing that there are any specified law for stalking is present or not. Many of the victims are not filing complaint or not lodging FIR because of threat and fear. Victims are fearing may be because of stalker's blackmailing, because of family reputation fear, society fear, mental fear etc. There are so many victims who are committing suicide in fear. So many victims are there who suffer with mental pressure and physical injury like acid attack and harassment etc. Because of the crime of stalking life of both accuse and victim gets damaged and both of them suffer. In this crime victims suffers a lot than accuse.

Indian Movies are portraying stalking in movies in a very cool way. There are a lot of movies in Tamil, Uttar Pradesh and Punjab and national movies in which stalking is shown very interestingly and often. People of the whole nation watch that movies and makes a type of perception in their mind may be some will get aware of that crime and not at all think to commit in life and some will think it as cool and that influences them to commit that crime further in life. In starting may be sometime they are also not aware that they are committing crime by stalking someone, they are troubling someone's life. There are so many peoples who will not try after stalking one time but there are some peoples also, who knows that he or she is not interested at all but then also they keep on stalking them because they are obsessive stalker. They are not at all ready to listen no they want to listen only, what they want and this thing provokes them to commit other heinous crime.

If Crime of Stalking is being done by someone for the first time then the accuse will get the bail in India. They do not have a sense of fear on first conviction. This is a loophole in the Law of stalking. Because there are chances that after getting bail from the court, accuse may commit some other crimes to take revenge from the victim. Other crimes like acid attack, rape, kidnapping, harassment and etc. If law does not grant bail to the criminals of Stalking on first conviction and strictly give punishment to them then there are chances that people will not commit the crime of stalking. It can create a kind of deterrence among peoples and stop them from committing the crime.

JUDICIAL DELAYS IN INDIA: A CONCERN WORTH ATTENTION

Author: Aditya Yadav, II year of B.B.A.,LL.B.(Hons.) from The Northcap University

A significant phrase well said by a British stateman and liberal politician William during a House of Commons debate on 16 March 1868. This phrase shows that if justice is not carried out timely, then even if it is carried out later it is not really justice because there was a period of time when there was a lack of justice, and the importance of that judgment is decayed as the time passes. This is presently used to define the major drawback of our judicial system. A common person is losing its faith for a less time-consuming court proceedings. There are various number of cases lingering for as more as 25 years and till date they are unable to get access for justice. In back late 18thcentury,the phrase was used as a suggestion for Israel to increase number of judges in its litigation and court proceedings but in present time its mainly used to show the poor performance and delay of our judicial system.

India is a county with almost 138 crores for population and as per the estimated research and studies it's been predicted that by 2023 India to become most populous nation[i] leaving behind China with almost 140.21 crores[ii]. Having a huge number of citizens there comes a greater number of disputes and cases and it require a strong judicial pillar for sustainable and proper judgement delivery and court proceedings.

MAJOR REASONS FOR DELAY OF CASES

I. Huge number of pending cases[iii]

Around 47 million cases are pending in courts in India, the government told parliament in March 2022. There were 70,154 cases pending in the Hon'ble Supreme Court and the number pending in the 25 high courts stood at 5,894,060 as of March 2022. Coming across this data we are able to see the real pressure and immense cases pending before our courts.

II. Shortage of various human and infrastructural resources

1. JUDGES AND JUDICIAL OFFICERS: hopelessly inadequate number of judges are undoubtedly one of the major reasons for case delays. Judge is one of the most decorated and respectful position throughout the world. As the will be no kind of judgement without a judge and is the core power and justice maker of the county. from the time of our independence decade by decade we are unable to fill up the post and vacancies for the judges. We are on our way to complete 75 years of independence on 15th august 2022 and developed but still hon'ble Supreme Court of India which is the supreme judicial authority of India and is the highest court of India. It has 30 Judges and a Chief Justice with cases pendency of 70,572 as of May 2, 2022[iv]. With a simple calculation almost 2,274 cases per a supreme court judge

is there. The pressure increases as going through the high courts, district courts and subordinate courts. We can easily get a clear idea of the pressure and workload on our judges, and it makes really hard for them to solve and dispose of the cases.

2. PHYSICAL INFRASTRUCTURE: As per the present records India have 1 Supreme court, 25 High courts, district courts or session courts and subordinate courts throughout the nation. In various courts mainly the subordinate and district level courts there are various infrastructural and management loopholes like lack of judicial infrastructure i.e. courtrooms, basic amenities which are required in a court by various court supporting staff, litigants, judges and also the court attendees. With a poor physical infrastructure, we are unable to accelerate proper functioning and disposal of cases.

3. SUPPORTING COURT STAFF: Beside the litigants arguing there matters and the judges hearing the same and passing orders and judgements and throughout this process there is a critical and predominant role and duties of the supporting court staff like the court officers, legal researchers, court clerks, as after the covid times online hearing and proceedings became prominent and necessary so various technical support team are required for smooth and unheddled court proceedings. Without these members and staff, it will be not possible for the courts to function.

III. DELAY AND PENDENCY ON BEHALF OF THE LEARNED COUNCILS

there are various myths and ideologies that judges are considered the main reasons of the delay of the cases in India. But going through my own research and observation I would state that the biggest reason for the delay of cases are the advocates and litigants. As courts have various procedures and steps which should be followed in particular cases and then are heard, and orders and judgements are passed. But the councils are not working properly according to the orders of the courts and the cases are lingers for a long time. Various negligence is seen on part of the advocates which are reason for the delay of cases proceedings like not well prepared with there cases and are unable to satisfy or explain their concerns and facts to the judges.Uncomplete pleadings like not filing written arguments, rejoinder, affidavit, and other legal documents which are needed for the proceedings of the cases are not on records and the case is unable to develop and remains pending.

Judges in various courts are working day and night restlessly under huge burden of cases and the amount of stress and pressure remains to be high and as there are less and inadequate number of judicial members in different courts resulting judges have to work extra by taking other benches and court hearings which ultimately increases there working time and burden of cases.

REMEDIES AND IMPROVEMENTS TO COUNTER THE PROBLEM OF PENDING CASES

I. The number of judges and judicial officers should be increased in The Hon'ble Supreme Court, high courts and other district and subordinate courts. Although we have highlyqualified and experienced judges, but their numbers are still low according to the present cases pending and on pilling up fresh cases it's important for the central and state government to boost the selection and placement of judges throughout the nation to distribute the cases and will fast forward the proceedings.

II.More number of Fast Track Courts should be set up along with proper and rigid directions that cases should be disposed offin a set time period. There is also a rising need to increase the number of tribunals and other judicial bodies which will help to reduces the burden of the courts. They should be supplied with adequate powers so that the litigants do not treat them like steppingstones to approach other Courts like High court or The Supreme court.

III. To avoid paperwork delays like posting of notices, hardcopy of cases files technological infrastructure like e-filing of cases, e- returnsand the case files must be stored online, which will help in both safety and speedy disposal of cases. The covid era have given it the adequate boost but further more development and awareness should be spread about the same.

IV. Cost and penalties should be imposed on the councils for various delays like late filing of various legal documents and adjournment should be limited and not be given on the cases where the councils are not following the procedure and the orders of the courts.

CONCLUSION

As the changes and solution of these problems can't be made over night but with constant attention and sincereness of our central and state government as well as the judicial bodies we will be able to have a well defined solution for the pendency of cases in different courts by proper appointment and working.

Author's Bio

Aditya Yadav is a 2st year student of B.B.A,LL.B from The Northcap University. His main interests are in corporate and criminal laws, highly adventurous and thrill seeking person.

CHAPTER NINE

SEXUAL HARRASMENT AT WORKPLACE

Author: Sneha Yadav, III year of B.A.,LL.B.(Hons.) from ICFAI University, Dehradun

Regardless of the occupation they hold, sexual harassment is a widespread issue that affects all women worldwide. However, because the legal system is inactive, nothing is done to protect these women. Not only that, but women who live in those nations with advanced legal systems also deal with issues like being dismissed from their jobs, being mocked, societal pressure, or promises of desired promotions, among others, they are therefore rendered speechless. It is used to remind women that they are weaker than males and is about male domination over women. The biggest obstacle to reducing sexual harassment in a culture where violence against women is used as a demonstration of the patriarchal ideals at play is due to these beliefs held by males. According to studies, sexual harassment affects one in three working women.[i]

This issue affects all nations today. No female employee is secure, and they lack a sense of security. Many nations' laws have undergone changes to better protect female workers from sexual harassment. 12,510 new allegations of workplace sexual harassment were filed with the U.S. Equal Employment Opportunity Commission and equivalent state agencies in 2007 alone.

Power dynamics at work make sexual harassment worse and are entrenched in cultural norms. Legal changes have little chance of being effective unless workplace sensitization is sufficiently emphasised. Workplaces must develop their own detailed procedures for handling sexual harassment. A system and a path for redress ought to be set up beforehand rather than putting committees together after the court gets involved.[ii]

India is a democratic country. Article 21 of the Indian Constitution states that everyone has the basic right to live with dignity. However, there is no statute that addresses sexual harassment expressly. Laws are unable to bring the victims justice. The Indian Supreme Court has heard a number of cases, but none of them have resulted in new statutes against sexual harassment. In Vishakha's case, the Supreme Court attempted to establish guidelines in 1997. These guidelines had some success since the Supreme Court in this instance claimed that distinct laws were necessary but that they weren't given the proper consideration.

Sexual harassment includes any unwanted physical, verbal, or non-verbal conduct of a sexual nature, including:[iii]

a) Physical contact and advances;

b) A demand or request for sexual favours;

c) Sexually coloured remarks;

d) Showing pornography; and

e) Any other sexually motivated behaviour, whether expressed directly or impliedly.

Laws that talks about Sexual harassment

Sexual harassment is prohibited under Indian law because it infringes on women's basic rights to equality with men and to live in dignity under articles 14 and 21, respectively. Although there are no particular laws in India to prevent sexual harassment at work, there are certain provisions in other pieces of legislation, such as the Indian Penal Code (IPC), which protects against sexual harassment of women[iv]:

- Section 294 addresses offensive behaviour and music in public spaces.
- Section 354 addresses physical or verbal violence against women
- Section 376 addresses rape
- Section 510 deals with speaking or acting in a way that offends a woman's modesty.

The legislature also approved the Indecent Representation of Women Act to further safeguard the rights of women (1997)[v]. Although sexual harassment cases have not been addressed by this legislation, several of its rules can be applied in one of two ways:

1) A person shall be subject to a minimum of two years in jail if they harass another by displaying books, pictures, paintings, videos, etc. that contain obscene representations of women.

2) This act's Section 7 penalises businesses that depict women in an indecent manner, such as by presenting pornography.

The harassed women may also file a lawsuit in civil court for torts including mental distress, physical abuse, loss of revenue from the victim's work, etc.

An example of quid pro quo sexual harassment is when a woman is harassed at work in exchange for advantages and sexual favours. This might result in punitive acts like demotion and having the woman work in challenging conditions. Another is "hostile working environment," which requires employers to create a welcoming workplace for female employees and forbids sexist graffiti, sexual comments that contain pornography, and brushing against female workers.

Indian case law on sexual harassment

The following cases were heard by Indian courts, and the verdicts in the majority of them encouraged women to file more complaints than they had in the past:

1) Apparel Export Promotion Council v. A.K Chopra[vi]

In this case, the Supreme Court ruled that sexual harassment is a form of gender discrimination against women and that any attempt or act of molestation by a superior qualifies as sexual harassment.

2) Mrs. Rupan Deol Bajaj v. Kanwar Pal Singh Gill[vii]

The definitions of modesty and privacy have been altered as a result of this case, making it illegal to harass or interfere with a woman's personal or professional life.

3) Vishaka & others Vs. State of Rajasthan & other[viii]

The Supreme Court established the following rules in this case, recognising both a private damage to a specific lady and a breach of her basic rights. These rules are important because they mark sexual harassment as a distinct type of illegal conduct for the first time. Until any additional law in this area is approved by parliament, these are applicable to all workplaces. These are the regulations

- Every company has a responsibility to give every woman employee a sense of security.
- The government ought to enact stringent laws and rules that forbid sexual harassment
- Any such behaviour should be met with disciplinary discipline, and the offender should also face criminal charges.

- The organisation should have a well-designed complaint procedure for the resolution of the victim's concerns, and it should be given a fair amount of time
- In order to prevent victims from feeling embarrassed while discussing their difficulties, this complaint process should take the shape of a complaint committee, which must be led by a woman and include at least 50% female members.
- In order to prevent victims from feeling embarrassed while discussing their issues, this complaint process should take the shape of a complaint committee, which must be led by a woman member and have at least 50% female committee members. A third party should participate in this complaint committee in the form of an NGO or other organisation with experience in this area. The government must receive an annual report from this committee as part of its demand for transparency in its operations.
- Sexual harassment-related topics shouldn't be taboo at employee meetings and should be openly discussed.
- The employer or the person in charge is obligated to take the necessary and reasonable steps to provide support to the victim of sexual harassment occurs due to the act or omission of a third party.
- The organisation is responsible for regularly informing female employees about their rights and the new guidelines issued and legislation passed.
- Employers in the private sector also need to abide by these rules; they are not just applicable to employers in the public sector.

4)Medha Kotwal Lele & ors. v. Union of India & Ors[ix]

This lawsuit aided Vishakha's case in effectively implementing the recommendations by notifying all states and union territories to provide the appropriate instructions.

Legislation to stop sexual harassment

The first attempt to develop appropriate draught law was done after a few years after the Supreme Court's rules, with significant input from and pressure from women's organisations. The 2005 "Protection against Sexual Harassment of Women Bill" was known as this. But even it fell by the wayside before being superseded by the "protection of women from sexual harassment at workplace bill, 2007,"[x] which put a special emphasis on workplace SH because the 2005 bill was considered too broad and so difficult to administer. Because it defines aggrieved women as "...any female/persons, whether major or minor, who allies that she/they have been victim to sexual harassment," this 2007 measure was not in the spirit of Vishakha. Additionally, there is no mention of third-party harassment in this legislation, which primarily emphasises workplace harassment. In contrast to the Vishakha guideline, which authorised criminal processes for the same, this bill regards sexual harassment as a civil issue. Section 12 (1) of the draught bill, which stipulates that "if the charges of sexual harassment are proved to be untrue, the complainant might be penalised for it," has recently undergone changes. This clause will provide employers a new opportunity to falsify the facts in order to discriminate against women. . Because of the concern that their employers would retaliate against them, it will discourage women from filing complaints against the perpetrator. Therefore, this sentence has to be removed. The aforementioned recommendations can help the vishakha guidelines keep their original intent, but they must also make sure that its reach doesn't grow too wide and raucous.

<u>Ineffective enforcement of the legislation against sexual harassment</u>

Every workplace is required by the vishakha standards to establish a complain committee, however private businesses seldom do so and governmental institutions only do it on paper. The organisations where these committees function have additional major issues since victims have complained that the committee members aren't even aware of their authority, duties, and obligations, which makes it difficult for the victim to receive justice. The employer's mentality is well ingrained since they assume that anything like this cannot occur in their workplace, which is why the women's complaint goes unanswered. People used to make fun of her, which prevented her from receiving justice or a fair hearing. The criminal provisions used in the majority of sexual harassment cases are sections 354 and 509 of the IPC, although these laws are only partially effective (as evidenced by the Mrs. Rupan Deol Bajaj v. Kanwar Pal Singh Gill decision). As a result, we may conclude that workplace sexual harassment is not strongly prohibited by law. There have been several measures developed (by the national commission for women, women's organisations, and the government)[xi], but it is still unclear which one will best accomplish the goal. The Ministry of Women and Child Development is now debating the proposed Protection of Women against Sexual Harassment at Workplace, 2007 document. Women's organisations have proposed the following ideas to amend the legislation:

- To offer members of the complaints committee procedural training.
- To amend Sections 11 (no action will be taken if the accusation against the respondent is untrue) and 12 (action will be taken against the complainant if a local committee determines that the allegation against the respondent is false) of the Agreement.

<u>Measures to Prevent Sexual Harassment</u>

1. A fundamental prerequisite for the implementation of any law protecting women in society is a shift in public opinion. By putting legislation into effect, unwanted sexual activity is protected. All levels of workers should practise sexual harassment prevention, and it should be ensured that female employees work in a supportive atmosphere. We advise taking the following actions in order to prevent sexual harassment at work.

2. Women should be encouraged to report sexual harassment if they feel it is affecting them in any way and invited to do so. They should be made aware that their complaints won't be laughed at or threatened in any way.

3. The employer should constantly be afraid of any financial or reputational loss that may result if this sort of action takes place in his organisation. Additionally, we believe that a distinct anti-sexual harassment policy should be developed that specifically addresses this problem.

4. The committee must always be fair while dealing with different members of the organisation.

5. A well-established mechanism for complaints that is in direct contact with the female employee should exist. Women shouldn't be embarrassed to voice their complaints about the difficulties they are having at work. The complaint committee should treat any complaint of this nature seriously, and action must be done in a timely manner.

6. Women employees should not be afraid to report any sex-related harassment, and it is their responsibility to notify the complaint committee right away of any such behaviour.

7. The complaint committee has a responsibility to keep every complaint private.

8. Every organisation ought to educate both male and female employees on sexual harassment. Employee comfort is increased and a hostile environment is helped by the mutual learning. The effects of sexual harassment on women ought to be covered in this training as well.

9. For the rules and procedures developed against sexual harassment to be successfully implemented, a commitment is needed from all levels of the organisation.

10. Every worker needs to be aware that it is his legal obligation to give every female employee a sense of security at work.

11. He should be aware that any harassment of his female employee will have a negative impact on her well-being, self-esteem, and potential at work, as well as lead to her quitting her position.

<u>**Conclusion**</u>

In India, workplace sexual harassment is a major problem, thus it's important to give female employees a supportive environment. Separate legislation should be passed by the government to address this problem. It should be aware that women workers make up a significant portion of the working population in India, and that it is the responsibility of the government to ensure their safety at work. Employers and managers need to devise new tactics to safeguard the company against this threat. Government and employers should make sure that women are treated equally and that there is no gender discrimination at work. The emergence and mutilation of sexual harassment may be minimised with effective policy implementation. By observing other organisations' tactics, one organisation can modify its strategy for dealing with sexual harassment. This will lessen or end the hiccups brought on by this damaging offence. Government should be aware that while separate laws may not result in gender equality, a legislation against sexual harassment would greatly aid women in their fight. Finally, we want to stress the importance of women not accepting things as they are since it is now necessary to speak up against all forms of injustice done to them.

Social acceptability is very important factor for dealing with these cases. There should be no shame or hesitation among the victim women's to come forward and tell the society about their problems they faced. Awareness among the public to speak up against this kind of act should be made so that they can become courageous enough to speak up for themselves.

CHAPTER TEN

MARITAL RAPE: AN UNADDRESSED STIGMA

Author: Riya Maggu, II year of B.A.,LL.B.(Hons.) from SRM University, Sonipat, Haryana, Delhi-NCR

Co-author: Vandana, II year of B.A.,LL.B.(Hons.) from SRM University, Sonipat, Haryana, Delhi-NCR

Martial rape doesn't become a rape....

They say, and why would it be?

Since, He had posted a logo of his surname on her

Body!!!

In India, if rape against woman is committed by an outsider it is considered as a criminal offence under Section 375 of Indian Penal Code but if that outsider is the husband of the woman and he raped her whilst being married, then what will be the scenario! Perhaps not the same as usual, he would not be called as rapist nor he would get punished because he is the husband and on top of that they are married. From thousands of years marriage is known to be one of sacred social institution binding a man and woman lifetime, but here we have this institution being questioned in court of law and whole this notion is connected with marital rape. Marital rape is one of the forms of crime committed against a woman in a four walled house and that too goes unreported.

At the basic outset, any law is valid if it withstands with test of constitutionality. There is no provision in Indian law that talks about the criminalization of marital rape. The supreme court of India as well as the high courts at the present moment are flooded with writ petitions demanding criminalization of marital rape and challenging the constitutionality of Exception 2 mentioned in Section 375 of Indian penal code (IPC). In light, of this ongoing stigma this article critically analyses the concept of marital rape and its constitutionality.

INTRODUCTION

Marital rape means if a wife has been coerced by the husband to engage in sexual relations with him without her consent and she is in a compromising situation that she can't even debate against it she has been raped by her own husband. A rapist remains a rapist irrespective of the relation he has with woman and same implied here too, if the husband is the one who has raped his wife, then he is a rapist he too deserves a punishment for same like all other crimes. At present only 150 countries have criminalized the marital rape and unfortunately India is not included in the set of these 150 countries because it yet hasn't criminalized the marital rape. Though, the countries recognized rape as an offence against a woman and have given the penalties for the same but they don't consider marital rape as one form of the rape committed against a woman just because they are in a marital relationship with each other. Now the main theme as to why we are debating a whole lot about it is that: Why India hasn't criminalized it yet? Well, the answers to this can many andjustificationshave been given by different thinkers and scholars at different points of time, and some of them are:- Firstly, it is believed that once a woman gets married to a man, it is considered that she has become a servile to her husband and is bound by his choices,no matter what she feels, because husband is the one who earns for the family, fulfil their basic needs and desires and wife has to obey husband's order. Secondly, there is a pre-assumption in society that when two adult individual gets married a husband has all rights over his wife physically, mentally, bodily in implied terms and it doesn't matter if wife has expressly told him so or not, here we can see the mindset of society that what it's all about as there is belief that marriage is based on consensus ad idem. Third, and most recent in trend is that court should not interfere into the private matters concerning husband and wife i.e their marital relations. It is the area of concern for a husband and wife that what is going on in their private relationship so court has no right to infer into that matter and this will be the infringement of their right of privacy.Now, its about court not interfering in the personal space of husband and wife and on other hand we question same in court of law and in this manner, this will not work out. Even the basic principle of doctrine of coverture treats husband and wife as single one identity and as so one cannot rape oneself. Shocking, isn't it? The main core of the issue in the way of criminalizing marital rape is that if it is criminalized, then it will destroy the basic essence of institution of the marriage and its impacts on Indian society will be long lasting.Secondly, in case if it is criminalized, then on what grounds it will be proven in court of law that how it is a valid and genuine case. Even on medical basis, it will be next to impossible to prove the guilt and further it may be used by the wife to threaten her husband in caseany dispute between them happens.

SITUATION: PAST AND PRESENT

Indian society is patriarchal in nature where male members of society are considered superior than female. Since the time immemorial, this system is being followed in our country which gives rise to male chauvinism. Somehow, this led to women being subjected to various forms of discrimination and exploitation that can be in different form and one of such atrocities which women have to go through is termed as marital rape. In India, there is cultural and social pressure due to which women tolerate it in silence and thousands of cases left unreported. But after all these incidents,victim has to live with her rapist just because he is her husband and this gives him rights to make sexual relationship without her free consent. According to the Indian government's latest family heath survey about 30% India women aged 18-49 reported having experienced spousal violence, the average Indian women is 17 times more likely to face sexual violence from her husband than from anyone else. Basically, its roots were installed at time of colonial period with emergence of case Phulmoni Devi, which attracted the attention of general public at large level in the year 1881. In this case, Phulmoni Devi, an eleven-year-old child bride, died due to excessive bleeding when her own husband, Hari Mohan, who was in his mid-thirties, tried to consummate their marriage despite his wife being eleven years old. As a result, this incident made to get the recognition of martial rape, although at small scale and made authorities to formulate laws such as Age of consent act 1861. The report of Verma committee also suggested the absolute and complete criminalization of the marital rape, stating that, the right to life.

Now, coming to present scenario the situation is still the same but a ray of hope has been given to people in one of the recent judgements of Karnataka High Court in Hrishikesh Sahoo vs State of Karnataka where it refused to quash a rape complaint registered against a husband by his wife who was accused of treating his wife as a "SEX SLAVE", well the word sounds horrific in itself, isn't it? While holding the rape complaint against the husband High court said"A man is a man; an act is an act; rape is a rape, be it performed by a man the 'husband' on the woman 'wife'. If it is punishable to a man, it should be punishable to a man albeit, the man being a husband."

Though, the fired topic has attracted attention of many since the year 2015 in which a petition was filed in Delhi high court to criminalize the marital rape. Thereafter, in August 2017, Central govt says criminalizing marital rape would destabilize the social structure of society and create a social deviance.

Even in the verdict given by Karnataka high court (march 2022), Justice M Nagaprasaanna criminalized the marital rape stated that institution of marriage cannot be used to confer any special male privilege or a license for unleashing of a "brutal beast" on the wife." A brutal act of sexual assault on the wife, against her consent, albeit by the husband, cannot but be termed to be a rape. Such sexual assault by a husband on his wife will have grave consequences on the mental sheet of the wife, it has both psychological and physiological impact on her such acts of husbands scare the soul of the wives."

Even though,Britain, who's political and constitution structure India is still following has already criminalized it.The united nation has also encouraged the countries around the globe to end up the marital rape by stating that "the home is one of the most dangerous place for women"[i]

EXCEPTION AND THE INDIAN LAW

Section 375 of Indian penal code (IPC) defines the offence to rape as: "sexual intercourse with a woman against her will, without her consent, by coercion, misrepresentation or fraud or at a time when she has been intoxicated or duped, or is of unsound mental health and in any case if she is under 18 years of age."[ii]Exception 2 to Sec 375 IPC states that: "Sexual intercourse by a man with his own wife, the wife not being under fifteen years of age, is not rape."[iii] The section itself considers rape as an offence against a woman but not in case where the there is a consensualsexual act between a husband and wife, since the crux of this whole act is based on the mindset of the marital relation between husband and wife. But on the other side law criminalizes marital rape concept under Section 376A of IPC which says that: "Whoever has sexual intercourse with his own wife, who is living separately from him under a decree of separation or under any custom or usage without her consent shall be punished with imprisonment of either description for a term which may extend to two years and shall also be liable to fine." [iv]It is a crime if man and woman are living separately but not if they are living together and the reason as to why this is so its because the society thinks that way and mindset of society affects our law system be it directly or indirectly. This exception under section 375 is discriminatory in nature as it forbids the married women to be exercise their rights as there is no such obligation in case of unmarried women.

In its 172[nd] law report the law commission of India[v]did talk about the issue of criminalizing marital rape but as always ignored the question and state that the criminalization of the same "may lead to excessive interference with marital relationship" [vi]and can destroy the institution of marriage. But however, the question here arises that- is marriage that type of contract or an institution that gave the husband right to engage into a non-consensual sexual intercourse with his wife? Well according to us the answer is no, but for society it is yes. In 17th century, England, Sir Mathew Hale said in one of his judgements that "the husband cannot be guilty of rape committed by himself upon his wife ,for by their mutual consent stand contract, the wife hath given up herself this kind unto her husband which she cannot retract"[vii] and the same thing goes for the Indian context too when Former CJI Deepak Mishra held that "I don't think that marital rape should be regarded as an offence in India, because it will create absolute anarchy in families and our country is sustaining itself because of the family platform which upholds family values"[viii]from following statements given by the justices itself it can inferred that why in India the concept of marital rape has not been criminalised yet.Keeping this thing in mind that everywhere whether it be the statement of a justice or be it the mindset of society the institution of marriage is given the first priority and this type of situation can't be interfered just because it is a sacred institution but at the same time there should not be any compromise with the fundamental rights of a women or particularly in context of this topic the wife. But here the statement seems a bit ironical because in Puttaswamy v. Union of India and The State of Maharashtra v. Madhukar Narayan[ix] supreme court ruled that sexual privacy is a fundamental right of all citizens and forced sexual act would be a clear violation of this right. In the cases of The State of Karnataka v. Krishnappa and The Chairman, Railway Board v. Chandrima Das, it was held that rape is a crime against the basic postulates of human rights and is an unlawful intrusion onto the right to privacy and sanctity of a female as guaranteed under Article 21[x].State says it can't interfere in the institution of marriage because it is a private matter but let's say there is an instance where a wife is subjected to cruelty or domestic violence in marriage then what will be the response of state to this…same as it held earlier, no it will be different because these two aspects are something which have already been criminalised so state have to take necessary steps to provide legal redress to the women. The concept of marital rape has yet not been criminalised so the matter is taken lightly as compare to the other ones.Perhaps, the tussle is still going in country as recently the Delhi high court gives a spilt judgement where Justice Rajiv Shakdher, who headed the two-judge Bench, struck down as unconstitutional the exception to Section 375 of the Indian Penal Code (IPC) which says that sexual intercourse by a man with his wife aged 18 or above is not rape even if it is without her consent. On the other hand, Justice C. Hari Shankar rejected the plea to criminalise marital rape noting that any change in the law has to be carried out by the legislature since the issue requires consideration of various aspects, including social, cultural and legal. Still the question remains unsolved, now it is totally on the discretion of Supreme Court to either criminalised it or not, on taking note of contemporary circumstances of Indian Society.[xi]

VIOLATIVE OF FUNDAMENTAL RIGHTS OF WOMEN

Article 14 states that "the state shall not deny to any person equality before the law or the equal protection of the laws within the territory of India". India is a diverse country with so many cultures inhabiting within the fold of this multi- ethnic society. So, our constitution provides for an equal set of opportunities to its citizens but at the very other side the provision contained in criminal law don't safeguard the women being raped by her own husband. The exception 2 to sec 375 of IPC has been proven to be discriminatory so far to article 14 because it doesn't provide the immunity to women against marital rape and at the same time doesn't provide for any type of punishment if he commits the same and continues to persuade the point that if two young adults are married then husband got every right on his wife even if it comes to point of raping her in order to fulfil his pleasures and lusts. The very base of this type of scenario is based on the existence of patriarchal society since decades and the gender-bias society.

Albeit, Article 15 of Indian constitution forbids discrimination on grounds only of religion, race, caste, sex, or place of birth. Then the question arises, why it is discriminatory in case when it came to address the rights of married women in scenario of marital rape.at the outset, her voice is being shut down on shake of societal prejudice and values?

As per the constitution of India, every citizen of India possesses fundamental rights such as article 21 of the Indian constitution clearly mentions that "protection of life and personal liberty" where the ambit of personal liberty also includes right to live a dignified life. Then the question of fact rises, why this right is not available to married women who is subjected to marital rape? Even in many debates the issue raised is that to what extend exception 2 to section 375 IPC is valid? This exception clearly mentions any sexual act performed by the man on his own wife is not rape as long as the wife is not a minor. The minister of state for home affairs Hari Bhai Parthiban Chaudhary said in 2015," the concept of marital rape, as understood internationally, cannot be suitably applied in the Indian context due to various factors, including levels of education, illiteracy, poverty, myriad, social customs and values, religious beliefs and mindset of the society to treat the marriage as a sacrament".

CONCLUSION

Is it truly fair to not punish a man for being the rapist of her own wife and truly justified to not give the dignity and respect back to those hundreds of women who have beenraped by their own husband or may be will raped if this scenario continues? Women who have been subjected to this crime have to remain with her aggressor under one roof and also have many long-lasting effects that can affect her mentally, physically and emotionally. So, keeping this instance in mind there is an urgent need to address this issue and criminalize the same. But we have come across types of cases where our laws have been misused by people to threaten other people for their needs and what if same happens once marital rape is criminalized; would the scenario will change or will it remain the same. Well, exceptions are everywhere and here can be too when we would heard of news stating a wife has falsely alleged her husband of committing marital rape on her. Here, we have two dimensions of same that to uphold woman's dignity but at same time not make it subjected to misuse. So, in criminalizing lawmakers have to consider all pros and cons of it. Moreover, there should be mutual understanding and both the parties involved, should respect the value of "consent" in the relationship.Therefore, at present, before criminalizing it, the basis of the ground to prove the marital rape should be taken in account. As legalizing it, will provide the unenriched benefits to the wife, putting husband into suppressed situation. Even if the light is put on that post consequence of those 150 countries which criminalized the marital rape has to face severe challenges. So, in contemporary world, some new initiatives that can be technological wise and a broad understanding is being demanded from our society to accept the aspect of criminalization of marital rape.

CHAPTER ELEVEN

ANALYSIS OF UNIFORMITY IN INDIA WITH RESPECT TO UCC UNDER ARTICLE 44 OF THE CONSTITUTION

Author: Sarthak Kulshrestha, III year of B.A.,LL.B. from Jagran Lakecity University, Bhopal

Introduction

The issue of the Uniform Civil Code surfaces in the news very frequently, but still, we see no development with regard to the implementation of the same. This implies that it is not that easy for the authorities to bring a UCC to India considering various irregularities and oddities in our country. Uniform Civil Code is explicitly mentioned in the Directive Principles of State Policy (DPSP) under Article 44 of the Constitution. Then, what must be the reason for the inability of the government to bring UCC to India? Before having taped the answer to this question, we need to understand what Uniform Civil Code, exactly is.

Uniform Civil Code is the way of bringing uniformity in India regarding the subjects which the different personal laws deal with, such as marriage, inheritance, maintenance, adoption, etc. The UCC has the object of replacing these personal laws with a single law to deal with the above-mentioned subjects. This aims to bring uniformity to India and make it hassle-free for the people and the authorities to deal with the matters as it would be based on a single set of rules. The entire concept sounds progressive, but the irregularities which are connected to it and the controversies related to the same act as impediments to bringing up the

UCC. This article deals with the technicalities of the issue and relevant case laws on the topic.

Historical background

India was a British colony and the English laws were made and implemented throughout the territory of India. The control over the governance of India was in the hands of the Crown since 1858. Having said that, it was wise for the British not to interfere with the cultural or religious aspects of our country in order to devise laws for the Indian populace so that the conflicts could be avoided and peace be maintained. So, no uniform law was enacted regarding the subjects for which personal laws or customs were already existing. In 1941, following the controversy on several legislations passed for the benefit of the Hindu women, a committee called B.N Rau committee was formed which had to examine the necessity of common Hindu laws. The committee recommended a common Hindu code which was debatable and finally after being lapsed once, it was resubmitted in 1952.

Passage of the Hindu Code bill

Hindu code bill was passed following a lot of discussion, and it was passed in four separate parts:

- Hindu Marriage Act, 1955
- Hindu Succession Act, 1956
- Hindu minority and Guardianship Act, 1956
- Hindu Adoption and Maintenance Act, 1956

The Hindu Code bill was passed but a big question that was pertinent to ask here is that why only Hindus are codified and not the entire population belonging to different religions is getting a uniform law? The government argued that it was done as a trial attempt to bring a code on personal matters for Hindus exclusively. If it would succeed, the other communities would ask for reconsideration of a code for themselves.

Incorporation of UCC in the Constitution?

The then Prime Minister Pt. Jawaharlal Nehru, accepted that the Hindu Code bill was incomplete in its stature as its implementation and formation had loopholes. Along these lines, he found Uniform Civil Code essential to include it in the Constitution. He hesitated to enforce UCC on diverse communities so as to avoid any conflict or chaos that's why he inserted UCC under Article 44 as a DPSP making it a non-justiciable directive.

Idea of uniformity through Uniform Civil Code

Article 44 of the Constitution states that the State shall endeavor to secure for the citizens a Uniform Civil Code throughout the territory of India. It ensures uniformity among all the citizens in dealing with the subjects such as marriage, inheritance, adoption, maintenance, divorce, etc. irrespective of the religion to which one belongs. The law will be uniform for all. Article 44 intends to leave no communal exception notwithstanding any existing personal law.

The idea is to bring uniformity in India to make all the citizens obliged to follow only one law in personal matters. The preamble to our Constitution characterizes India to be a secular democratic republic nation. Considering the secular nature of India, it seems to be imperative for our country have a uniform law on personal subjects for the citizens so that it would ensure no bias or inequalities as such voids are present in the personal laws. Some of the advantages of UCC are as follows:

Equal status to all citizens

In the contemporary times of India, the biased behavior among the citizens who belong to different and diverse backgrounds is not at all suitable. It acts as an obstacle in the collective development of the society. But the introduction of a common code for civil and personal matters without any bias based on religion, caste, class, gender, etc. will be certainly helpful to ensure equal status to every citizen of the country.

Elimination of gender bias

The existing personal laws for both Hindus and Muslims are considered to be highly discriminatory against women. Whether it be the maintenance, inheritance, or any other issue, it is the woman who suffers much more complications and trouble than a man under the personal laws. It is observed that men are granted upper preferential status in matters of succession and inheritance. But, a gender neutral uniform civil code would eliminate all the discriminatory aspects and will ensure gender parity in its proviso in every subject.

A boon for young population of India

In India, the youth forms around 50% population, i.e. is up to 25 years of age. This constitutes a large part of the Indian population. They are witnessing the contemporary changes in the society and seeing the rise in the level of significance of the principles like equality, humanity, social welfare, modernity, etc. These principles are believed to vehemently oppose the gender inequalities, detrimental approaches towards the interpretation of religion, etc. So, uniform civil code would be beneficial as well as relevant for them to cast uniformity in India in personal matters in accordance with the progressive principles of modern day society.

Support the integrity of the nation

The way in which the principle of rule of law keeps all the citizens equal in the eyes of law, the same should be the case with the issues on personal as well. If there would be no different personal laws and everyone would be obliged to follow a common code for certain subjects, then the object of national integrity could be achieved easily.

Challenges in the implementation of UCC

Although there is the need of uniform civil code in India, but there are practical challenges that the government faces in the implementation of UCC in India. A major challenge is the tussle between the idea of uniformity under Article 44 and Article 25 of the Indian Constitution.

Article 25 of the Indian Constitution guarantees every citizen, the fundamental right to freely profess, practise and propagate religion. The argument given by the people challenging the Uniform Civil Code is that UCC is against the fundamental right to religion which is guaranteed under Article 25. The UCC seeks to dissolve the personal laws which is seen as an attack on Article 25 by some people, especially the minorities. They also contend that Article 44 is only a Directive Principle of State Policy, a non-justiciable right and it is not enforceable in courts but Article 25 is a Fundamental Right which is enforceable in courts. Article 25 empowers the State to regulate or restrict the secular activities and the religion has nothing to do with those matters. So, the matters of inheritance, maintenance, adoption, divorce, etc. are the ones which are to be dealt with law and not by religion. The challenge in the introduction of UCC is highly driven due to the insecurity of the minorities. Another major reason of insecurity which the minorities feel is the imposition of Hindu personal laws under the garb of Uniform Civil Code. These are some of the reasons or the misinterpretation of Article 44 in minds of minorities which prevent this important step towards the social development of the Indian society.

Present status of Uniform Civil Code in India

In India, there only one state where Uniform Civil Code is enforceable by law and that is Goa. Goa was a colony of Portugese until 1961 when it became a part of India by Daman & Diu Administration Act, 1962. Goa has the UCC but it is much different than what Article 44 and the State perceives it to be.

The Goa Civil Code lets the parties to a marriage sign a contract to complete its solemnization. After marriage the property of both husband and wife becomes common and there are equal rights on ancestral property of both sons and daughters. There also exist some loopholes in Goa civil code such as the Hindu men are given the right of polygamy in case the wife is unable to conceive a child till the age of 25 or a male child till 30 years of age. And Muslim men cannot engage in polygamy if they don't get their marriage registered under the code. There are differences between the registration of marriage for Catholics and non-Catholics.

So, there are various irregularities in the Goa Civil Code too, therefore it can't be said to be a uniform law. It lacks the ability to achieve the objectives of a uniform law such as gender equality, equal rights of the parties on a subject of personal matter, etc.

<u>Relevant case laws</u>

The Supreme Court and state High Courts have, in many instances, recommended the government to bring UCC. The judiciary has at times, recognized UCC to be the need for our country. Some of the relevant case laws are as follows:

Mohammed Ahmed Khan v. Shah Bano Begum (1985)

In this case, the husband of Shah Bano Begum took divorce from her and she was denied her claim for maintenance in the High Court. But the Supreme Court ruled in the favor of her and held that she is entitled to maintenance u/s 125 of Cr.P.C. Further, the Supreme Court held that a pending document, UCC must be finally enacted. It will help to resolve the conflicts between different ideologies by removing disparate loyalties to the personal laws. The Honorable Supreme Court accepted the difficulties to bring various communities under the purview of a single and uniform law, but it said that a beginning has to be made if the Constitution has to have any meaning.

Ms. Jorden Diengdeh v. S.S. Chopra (1985)

In this case, the Supreme Court observed that the personal laws are not uniform and do not comply with the principles of equality. The laws related to divorce and judicial separation have flaws in them and uniformity must be there to deal with the cases on these subjects. This could be done by introducing UCC in the country so that these matters can be addressed fairly irrespective of religion or gender.

Sarla Mudgal v. UoI (1995)

In the given case, the Supreme Court held that conversion to Islam and marrying again would not, by itself dissolve the Hindu marriage. Thus, second marriage solemnized after converting into Islam would be an offence u/s 494 of the IPC. The SC again said that the UCC should be retrieved from the cold storage and enforced by India.

Shayara Bano v. UoI (2017)

The recent case of Shayara Bano is highly relevant as it entails the need of UCC as the Supreme Court considered while deciding the constitutional validity of triple talaq practice of divorce by Muslim men. The Court held triple talaq to be unconstitutional and laid emphasis on the uniform civil code to eliminate such unjustified practices in personal laws.

Conclusion

The introduction of the Uniform Civil Code in India will, no doubt, prove to be fruitful for the citizens and the nation as a whole. But it is difficult in the Indian scenario considering various cultural, religious and other differences. It is a progressive law and such a law should be brought in a suitable atmosphere where it can be successfully implemented. As directed by the Apex Court in numerous instances, India needs UCC and it will serve the social development of our country. A lot of times, the idea of UCC is denigrated due to the possible violations of the same considering that India is not that foolproof to follow the intended proviso of the code. This is a very weak argument because just due to the reason of a possible violation of a law, a developmental law should not be stopped from implementation.

Also, when the Hindu Code Bill was brought, it created a lot of chaos through the protests. But, it was accepted and in a similar fashion, UCC would be a law aiming at the long-term welfare of the citizens. This has to be considered seriously to bring the diverse population under the umbrella of a common-law so that gender-neutral and developmental objectives of UCC could be achieved.

CHAPTER TWELVE

IPR: PATENT WAIVER AND INDIA'S SURGE IN MAKING COVID VACCINES

Author: Pranavi Challa, I year of B.A.,LL.B. from Trinity Institute of Professional Studies, Dwarka

Abstract

As the toll of COVID-19 continues to extend in several countries within the world, there has been a revived push to deal with the matter of immunogen deficiency through a relinquishment of patent rights. The concern regarding waiver has continued through the pandemic, from formal proposals introduced in 2020 by a number of large developing countries like India and South Africa, through media, editorials in scientific publications, like Nature. This push gained momentum in 2021 before the meeting of the Trade Organization's General Council.[1]

This paper tries to elucidate the legal problems surrounding the "TRIPS WAIVER" which is being supported by sixty nation states at international level. Focusing on the patent rights and trade secrets- that squarely is relevant to this COVID-19 immunogen context. This will lead to drafting a case as why the prevailing journey flexibilities around the mandatory licensing square measure incapable of addressing this pandemic context adequately, in terms of each procedure and legal substance.

Introduction

In order to understand the main problem of Patent Waiver, it is first necessary to understand the basic concept of IPR (Intellectual Property Rights) and the principles of patent and trade secrets.

What is Property[2]

The objects which are legally recognized as having either an individual or a group are called property. This also includes," a right of ownership". They are of two types: (a) Tangible Property: which has some form of physical form. For example, Building, land, house. (b) Intangible Property: which includes the mental effort of an individual or group and does not include any form of physical substance.

Intellectual Property

It is an intangible or incorporeal property (which is something a person has ownership of that can be transferred to another person but does not include physical substance.)

Intellectual Property Rights

Intellectual Property Rightsare defined as the rights given to the people over the creation of their minds or for their mental labor. Rights include legal, social, or ethical entitlement about what is allowed to be used by the legal system.

1. Copyright

It is a type of intellectual property derivedfrom creative work that gives its owner exclusive rights for a limited time. It includes literary, artistic, musical, and many more. It prohibits any other person or institution from producing, distributing, or publicly performing the particular work.

2. Trademark

The basic rule contained in Article fifteen is that any sign, or any combination of signs, capable of identifying the products and services of one enterprise from those of different undertakings, should be eligible for registration as a trademark, providing it's visually perceptible. Such signs, above all words together with personal names, letters, numerals, figurative components and mixtures of colors further as any combination of such signs, should be eligible for registration as emblems.

3. Trade Secrets

Undisclosed business information that has an economic or commercial value derived from its [3]secrecy.The issue of trade secrets continues to be the item preventing an accord. Trade secrets within the scope of any scientific discipline relinquishing argue that it'll not be doable to copy a number of the vaccines on the premise of the knowledge disclosed within the patents alone.

Pharmaceutical corporations' area unit troubled concerning what is going to happen to their trade secrets associate in nursing different lead once any time-limited vaccinium relinquishing involves a finish. The key church doctrine of the law of trade secrets is within the name –the knowledge the data} should be secret – and once any information is disclosed then it's unfeasible to undo this later.

4. Patent

[i]An exclusive right granted for the invention of a particular product or the process that provides a way to a new solution. It is a legal right that allows its owner to make, use or sell his own invention.

According to the WTO; The visits Agreement needs Member countries to create patents offered for any inventions, whether or not product or processes, all told fields of technology while not discrimination, subject to the traditional tests of novelty, creative thinking and industrial pertinence. It's conjointly needed that patent be offered and patent rights pleasurable while not discrimination on the place of invention and whether or not product square measure foreign or regionally created (Article twenty-seven). There square measure three permissible exceptions to the fundamental rule on patentability.

One is for inventions contrary to order public or morality; this expressly includes inventions dangerous to human, animal or plants or health or seriously detrimental to the setting. the employment of this exception is subject to the condition that the business exploitation of the invention should even be prevented and this hindrance should be necessary for the protection of order public or morality (Article twenty-seven).

The second exception is that Members could exclude from patentability diagnostic, therapeutic and surgical ways for the treatment of humans or animals (Article twenty-seven).

The third is that Members could exclude plants and animals apart from micro-organisms and basically biological processes for the assembly of plants or animals apart from non-biological [4]and microbiological processes. However, any country excluding plant varieties from patent protection should give a good single system of protection. Moreover, the entire provision is subject to review four years when entry into force of the Agreement (Article twenty-seven).

The exclusive rights that have got to be bestowed by a product patent square measure those of creating, using, giving available, selling, and commercialism for these functions. method patent protection should offer rights not solely over use of the method however conjointly over product obtained directly by the method. Patent house owners shall even have the correct to assign, or transfer by succession, the patent and to conclude licensing contracts (Article 28).

Vaccine Patent

Parents are important for the vaccine as it prevents competitors from simply copying the company's discovery and launching a rival product. In India, patents on pharmaceuticals typically last for 20 years from the date it was filed. Usually, getting a vaccine approval takes decades, but in extreme conditions like COVID-19, it took around two months to acquire the patent.

Importance of Patent Protection to the drug manufacturers

As it takes years of blood and sweat for many researchers to develop a vaccine. It involves a lot of expense during years of laboratory, animal, and human testing, with the prospect of years of sale without competition.

WTO DECISION ON PATENT IN 2003

WTO agreed on 30 August 2003 to make legal changes so that even the economically weaker countries can import generic medicine, but on the condition of the compulsory licensing if they are unable to manufacture the medicines themselves.

In 2021, many countries have put forward a Patent Waive in regards to reducing or ceasing the compulsory licensing which would help many third-world counties to develop their own vaccines.

What is a Patent Waiver?

'Patent Waiver' is a proposal to abdicate certain provisions of TRIPS (Trade-Related Intellectual Property Rights) for a period of 3 years. TRIPS provides certain member countries to have certain intellectual property protection. This involves the decision taken in 2003 in which WTO, as well as TRIPS, made it mandatory for the third world countries to have license in order to adopt any foreign drugs in their native country. The three main options of the Agreement are:

- **Standards**

In respect of most areas of property coated by the Visits Agreement, the Agreement sets out the minimum standards of protection to be provided by every Member. most components of protection are outlined, specifically the subject-matter to be protected, the rights to be presented and permissible exceptions to those rights, and also the minimum period of protection. The Agreement sets these standards by requiring, first, that the substantive obligations of the most conventions of the WIPO, the Paris Convention for the Protection of commercial Property (Paris Convention) and also the Bern Convention for the Protection of Literary and creative Works (Berne Convention) in their most up-to-date versions, should be complied with. With the exception of the provisions of the Bern Convention on ethical rights, all the most substantive provisions of those conventions are incorporated by reference and therefore become obligations beneath the visits Agreement between visits Member countries. The relevant provisions are to be found in Articles a pair of.1 and 9.1 of the visits Agreement, that relate, severally, to the Paris Convention and to the Bern Convention. Secondly, the visits Agreement adds a considerable range of extra obligations on matters wherever the pre-existing conventions are silent or were seen as being inadequate. The visits Agreement is therefore generally cited as a Bern and Paris-plus agreement.

- **Enforcement**

The second main set of provisions deals with domestic procedures and remedies for the social control of material possession rights. The Agreement lays down bound general principles applicable to any IPR social control procedures. Additionally, it contains provisions on civil and body procedures and remedies, probationary measures, special necessities associated with border measures and criminal procedures, that specify, in an exceedingly certain quantity of detail, the procedures and remedies that has to be out there in order that right holders will effectively enforce their rights.

• 79 •

- **Dispute settlement**

The Agreement makes disputes between WTO Members regarding the respect of the visit's obligations subject to the WTO's dispute settlement procedures.

Concluding Remarks

To summarise, there's a powerful legal basis within the TRIPS agreement for granting of exceptions to the protection of IPRs so as to fulfil different public policy rationales like combatting a deadly disease or other national health emergencies. The Patent waiver is an essential for the mass production of the drugs to save lives in this drastic COVID period. WTO, During the period of the rising COVID deaths should issue a grant for this purpose.

CHAPTER THIRTEEN

ARTICLE 356: AGAINST PRINCIPLE OF CONSTITUTIONALISM

Author: Alok singh, II year of B.A.,LL.B. from University of Petroleum and Energy Studies

Meaning of constitutionalism: Before going into the arguments, we need to understand the meaning of constitutionalism. Constituionalism means that the power of the government should be limited and their actions should be free of arbitrariness, unfairness, and unreasonableness. There should be a negative restriction on the powers of the state. Then only can we say that a country is a welfare state. For good and democratic governance, it is very important to have the "rule of law" instead of rule by law. Then only can we say that the government is following the principle of constitutionalism. It is not important to have a constitution, but it is important to have "constitutionalism" because many countries have constitutions but there is still discrimination going on within their territory . Countries like Pakistan and China have the constitution but still have minorities within their countries being oppressed just because they do not have constitutionalism.

When president rule can be Invoked by article 356: Whenever president upon report of governor or otherwise is satisfied that constitution machinery in state has been failed then the president is having the power to impose president rule in a state.

History of article 356: Article 356 of India constitution traces its origin from section 93 of government of India act,1935.Britishers were also having the same power when they enacted the government of India act,1935.But after the independence of India framers of our constitution enumerated this provision into our constitution.

Against the principle of constitutionalism: Now let's talk about article 356 and how it is acting as an instrument of misuse and why it is against the principle of constitutionalism. Article 356 is all about the imposition of president's rule whenever the constitutional machinery of a state fails, but the question here is how we will determine the situation where constitutional machinery has failed.

Many times we have seen that the central government has not given any proper reason against the imposition of president's rule in a state.

In 1951, this provision was misused by the Nehru led government when they dismissed the government of Punjab Gopichand Bhargava even though they had a majority of states and there was no failure of constitutional machinery, but due to this vague government, they took an unfair advantage.

In the 1970's and 80's, it was very common for the government to impose president's rule in opposition rules states on the ground of this vague term, i.e., "failure of constitutional machinery".

Historically, this provision was highly misused during the regime of Indira Gandhi. When the Janta Party came into power and when they formed a government in the centre, they also imposed president's rule on 12 congress-ruled states. When Indira Gandhi came back to power, she again imposed president's rule on different states which were governed by janta party.This shows that article 356 has been a tool for political rivalry.

By looking at these instances, we can say that article 356 is a provision which is against the principle of constitutionalism because it does not limit the power of the government but rather gives the government authority to act in an arbitrary manner. When a provision is used by a government to exact political retribution, it means that the government has the authority to act arbitrarily.

Article 356 also gives the power to the government to "rule by law", which is not acceptable in a democratic country. A democratic country needs the "rule of law" to sustain constitutionalism.

Sakaria commission gave its report in which they mentioned about the ground of imposing article 356 or president rule but the government always wanted to act in a arbitrary manner that is why they never accepted the their recommendations and their action shows that the never to enhance constitutionalism.

According to article 51a of the Indian constitution, citizens of India are required to fulfil certain fundamental duties, one of which states that "we should respect the ideas that played a crucial role in our struggle for independence," and article 356 is incompatible with this fundamental duty because our freedom fighters never supported this type of provision, as a result of which the British government suspended section 93 of the Government of India.And by imposing such a kind of provision, we are not cherishing the ideas of our free leaders. Which again shows that this provision is against the principle of constitutionalism.

CHAPTER FOURTEEN

AGNIPATH FOR AGNIVEERS: A PATHWAY TO INDIAN ARMED FORCES

Author: Khyati Jain, II year of B.Com.,LL.B.(Hons.) from School of Law, JECRC University, Jaipur

Co-author: Prerna Singh, II year of B.Sc.,LL.B.(Hons.) from School of Law, JECRC University, Jaipur

Khyati Jain

Prerna Singh

INTRODUCTION

The government of India unveiled "Agnipath Scheme," on June 14th 2022, a defense reform initiative that had previously known by the name "Tour of Duty." The objective is to implement such reform is commendable because it defies stereotypes and helps in implementing urgently required needs in the army, navy, and air force. However, there are several issues and problems with the implementation of this scheme for both the soldiers and society as a whole such as little period of service, no pension given etc.[i]

It has received a lot of flak and condemnation. The concept was presented without prior discussion and was attacked by the opposition parties, defense analysts, farmers, and prospective army recruits for having a number of problems. The irate teenagers have vandalized government buildings, burned down buses, and damaged public property nationwide. In this blog, the researchers have discussed the need for this scheme, its repercussion and the issues raised by the people.

ABOUT THE SCHEME

The Agnipath system is intended for recruiting at all levels below commissioned officers and is applicable to all three branches of the armed forces: the Army, Navy, and Air Force. The plan would enroll Army recruits, who will be referred to as Agniveers. Agniveers will be enrolled on a "All India All Class" basis and not on the basis of regional and caste, this is also a major reason for the protest, and must adhere to the medical standards for enlisting. The educational requirement for becoming a General Duty (GD) soldier is Class 10. The eligibility criteria for the recruitment with respect to educational qualification has been given as 10th pass and 12th pass depends upon force to force. They can apply for various post such as technical, technical aviation, clerk and store keeper etc.[ii]

By September or October of 2022, applications for the programme will open, and it is anticipated that 45,000 to 50,000 people will apply. The recruitment is divided in majorly two parts, one is up to 25000 Agniveers will be recruited in the first half of December 2022 and by first half of February 2023, the remaining are recruited. The plan comprises recruiting young people for a four-year contract in military uniform in the age range of 17 and a half to 21. Of these four years, only six months would be devoted to training; the rest would be used for deployments, particularly those involving difficult operational tasks.[iii]

After the completion of the 4 years, only 25% of the most motivated and effective troops will be given the opportunity to extend their service with the military for 15 years. By the fourth year of the service term, Agniveers will receive about Rs 40,000 (monthly). The sufferer will, however, be the 75% who were excluded. The government will pay individuals who aren't chosen a severance of roughly Rs 11 lakh from a corpus fund at the time of leaving.[iv] However, they won't be able to take advantage of pension benefits like they could under the prior hiring policy. Additionally, those excluded will be jobless, and missing out on the job market for four years and it will be very difficult for them to survive and support their family with just a certificate of 12th pass in hand.

In the previous system, there was a minimum 15-year service requirement followed by a universal pension. Although the government claims to want a more youthful military, there may be other significant factors at play. The Army has two expenditures: capital and revenue, with capital accounting for 25% of total expenditures and income for 75% of them. Pension payouts are classified as a revenue expense. Additionally, the pension accounts for 25% of the $5.75 trillion total defense expenditure in FY23.[v] Therefore, the government plans to enhance the percentage of capital expenditure utilized to raise the quality of the armed forces by reducing a sizeable pension through this programme.

<u>CRITICAL ANALYSIS BENEFITS</u>

This radical departure from the established employment norms in the recruitment procedure for the three military forces would be brought about by the Agnipath Scheme. This scheme will also be opened for the women based on service requirements who had a wish to serve their life for nation.

As the goal is to lower the average age from 32 years to 26 years within the next four to five years, it will result in a younger military. Defense Minister Rajnath Singh explains that one of the main benefits of having a young military is that they can receive better training in cutting-edge technologies. Admiral R Hari Kumar said that there are women officers who are already deployed on frontline warships and the women sailors who become part through this scheme will provide armed forces with a "wider talent pool" and prove to be an asset.[vi]

The removal of pension benefits, which means that after four years of service, they will not receive a pension but will instead receive other advantages like the Seva Nidhi fund and tax exemption. The government has announced a 10% reservation for "Agniveers" in the Assam Rifles and central police services, with an upper age relaxation. The Coast Guard, defense civilian positions, 16 defense PSUs, including significant ones like Hindustan Aeronautics and Bharat Electronics, as well as four shipyards and 41 ordnance factories, will all be covered by the 10% quota that the Defense Ministry has proposed.

The Agniveers will receive a unique qualification certificate on the successful completion of their service, and the skills which they have acquired and the training that they have received will result in making them a better and more useful and obedient human resource for society. Last but not least, if soldiers choose to pursue higher education, their membership in the army, navy, or air force will be taken into account when determining their eligibility for financial aid. They will also receive a Class 12 equivalent certificate and bridging courses to help them continue their education.

CHALLENGES

Firstly, Agniveers recruits may find it extremely demotivating to work without a pension. Under prior recruitment system, the recruits had a 15-year service commitment and received a respectable pension for the rest of their lives. In this new scheme the recruits won't have the same degree of zeal and determination now that the service commitment will only be for 4 years and they will only be selected for additional service in 25% of cases. Given that the majority of these recruits come from low-income or middle-class families, the significance of pensions in their life cannot be understated. A major incentive for joining the armed forces is the financial security which they get from the government in the form of pension which helps to support their families. The feeling of Nationalism and patriotism don't exactly satisfy hungry stomachs, and for army recruits, the financial stability of their family is utmost importance given the danger to their life. Therefore, the government's cost-cutting initiatives shouldn't be at the expense of those who put their lives in danger to defend the country. Given India's volatile borders, the armed services are the last profession in the country that can afford any amount of demotivation.

Secondly, what will happen to the 75 percent of recruits who do not get chosen after serving their term? Although they will receive a lump sum payment of about 11 lakhs and a loan of up to 18.2 lakh over three years, would that be enough to provide for these recruits' and their families' met needs for the rest of their lives? What hope do 75% of Agniveers have with just a 12th standard pass certificate in hand and being unemployed for almost four years? Every year, 30,000 to 40,000 more individuals will become unemployed, and to make matters worse, they won't even have pensions to help them financially. Surely none of their military education or their 3.5 years of Army service will result in new employment. What would the risk and expense to society be if it had to deal with a military-trained, frantic army of unemployed young men? In April 2022, India's overall unemployment rate rocketed to 7.83 percent, and the future doesn't appear to be particularly promising either.

The third issue is the soldier's ability to learn new skills in six months of training as opposed to recruits to the normal cadre. Many things would depend on it, including the types of tasks they would fill because younger armed personnel cannot compromise on training, professionalism, or experience. If we look into the recruitment process of other countries- The Israeli military, one of the best in the world, has one of the shortest service requirements in the world, with men and women serving for 30 and 22 months, respectively. Short-term contracts are not exclusive to Israel; they also exist with the US, UK, and France. Therefore, it is necessary to assess both factors fairly.

The fourth issue is how the young soldiers will be able to reintegrate into society after serving in the armed forces because they won't feel any sense of patriotism or purpose in their regular occupations. Frustration, anxiety, and sadness could result from this. Since there are many potential outcomes associated with the flotation of this scheme, it is important to address all of the issues before moving forward with this reform.

The final issue is if the young soldiers would pose a threat to society once their four-year commitment is up because of their experience in battle and military training. This is because training young people in the use of weapons while they are in the military may serve as a deterrent for society since there may be an increase in incidences of violence by soldiers who have been prematurely discharged from the military and it will also be a very difficult task for the young soldiers who comes under 75% to live a normal life after serving four years in forces.[vii]

CONCLUSION

The military recruitment process has halted and severely affected from the last 2 years due to the COVID 19 pandemic which struck the nation. Even while not all of the vacancies will be filled through the Agnipath programme, it will still be a brave move in Indian history as it seeks to dismantle the centuries-old structure created by the British. This scheme seems as a second chance for those young minds who want to become part of forces but couldn't make it to the exam. This Scheme not only helps the young minds by giving them opportunity to serve nation but also if they are not selected in the 25% then with that money and the training of various technologies which they will receive can help them to start a startup and in the near future we will see some successful entrepreneur. The necessity for a smaller armed force is urgent given the heavy dependence on technology, such artificial intelligence, in battle. The militaries all over the world are attempting to minimize the number of soldiers while increasing spending on cutting-edge weapons.

Every reform has flaws and gaps that must be filled, especially when they relate to the nation's safety, defense, and security. To ensure the success of this programme, the government must resolve all issues raised by all parties engaged with the utmost honesty. The process has already started, with the government raising the age requirement to 23 years old as a one-time waiver for the year 2022 to include all individuals who were unable to apply over the previous two years because the recruiting procedure was delayed due to COVID. After violent protests broke out across the nation, this was done.

CHAPTER FIFTEEN

DATA PRIVACY ON SOCIAL MEDIA: AN INTERNATIONAL PERSPECTIVE

Author: Kartikey Arora, I year of B.B.A.,LL.B. from University School of Law and Legal Studies (USLLS), GGSIPU, Dwarka ,New Delhi

<u>INTRODUCTION</u>

In a technologically advanced, innovation driven world there is an endless list of apps and sites collectively termed as social media that provide with an interface to connect, communicate and interact with the world at large. It is not only restricted to allowing people to share their own thoughts and activities but also get to know more about other people through the concepts of following, followers, connections etc. Although this has a vast and diverse amounts of benefits but many at times amidst the lines of enhancing connections and the maximum utilization of social media, we often give away our fundamental and basic right of privacy. Data privacy in simple terms refers to the control and command that we have over our personal information i.e. name, date of birth, address, location etc.

Whenever we come across the terms of service of any social media app by clicking on 'I Agree' we essentially enter into a legal binding contract with the particular app or site. Now this contract does have a consideration which might be in terms of a fee in case of paid access, while in case of free access the cost of using the apps itself comes at a cost of infringement of the privacy of an individual. The prescribed social media app or site gets full rights to share the personal information of the user with any third-party for collecting data in terms of usage or for creating advertisements matching the needs of users.1This article analyses how data privacy today stands as a global threat and the laws put in force internationally to restrain the breach of privacy; along with the need to curb certain loopholes in such laws.

MAJOR PRIVACY ISSUES ACROSS THE GLOBE

In a world where social media presence has become almost as prevalent as consuming food for survival the number of users have grown by many folds in almost a span of 10 years in the 21st Century. In America, according to the Pew Trust statistics, the number of users has grown fourteen fold over the last decade. With this exponential growth in the number of users what has also significantly risen is the threat to data privacy. Crimes have also seen an immense escalation in terms of breach of privacy through social media apps by hacking accounts of people, stealing personal data and also infringing the privacy rights of their connections including friends, family, relatives etc.

About 13% of Americans have experienced unauthorized use of their data on social media platforms,while 9 out of 10 Canadians feel that their online information is prone to data breach;2 at the same time 79% of internet users across the world believe that they have lost control over their personal data.3 In such a scenario it is integral to bring to the knowledge of the readers as to what types of privacy issues are actually widespread to curb the threat of privacy breach. Following are few of the most important and popularly used methods through which the violation of data privacy is carried out:

1. Data Mining

Once a person willingly presses on "I agree" after going through terms of service and many at times ignoring it in order to quickly access the desired social media site or app, the app platform gains the right to do whatever it pleases with the private information cause as already stated it acts as a consideration in return fie providing free access to the app or site. This information can then be:

A. Shared with any third party

B. Shared with an advertising agency for the sake of advertising to targeted audience

C. Shared or stored in countries where privacy laws are lenient for e.g. people in Canada are concerned about their data being stored elsewhere outside their own country.

D. They can also share your photos and profile details integrating it with ads and promotions.

E. Used to influence your opinions, likes and dislikes as in the case of Cambridge Analytica when the data of millions of users in U.S & Canada where leaked by social media giants like Facebook in order to shape opinions and gain insights during 2016 U.S election campaign.

2. Privacy Setting Loopholes& Mergers

When using social media platforms, one might have come across a privacy setting that might provide an individual the assurance that they can bolster their data privacy providing a layer of protection. Despite this trend being prevalent in today's times, it acts more like a loophole rather than an advancement in terms of data protection. This is so because even when the privacy settings are turned on the posts, messages or information shared is accessible to the friend circles of the user sharing the same, many at times not many in the friend circle have privacy settings turned on which in turn result in the messages being within the reach of friends of those friend circles thus they can share it with almost anyone; making the privacy settings a futile instrument in the implementation of data privacy.

Another trend that has gained prominence over the recent times is the merger of social media platforms that acts as an inherent threat to data privacy as the companies tend to change their privacy policies. A prime example of this being the merger of WhatsApp an app that gave data privacy utmost priority, with social media giant Facebook. Back in 2012, the CEO of WhatsApp declared that they do not and will not share the data of their users with any third-party, consequently after the takeover by Facebook in

2014; it was declared that all the privacy policies of WhatsApp had to align with the parent company of Facebook which were much weaker compared to the prioritized privacy settings of WhatsApp originally. Thus infringing the privacy of millions of users across the globe.4

3. Phishing Attempts

One of the most common methods of private data hacking used by criminals and hackers throughout the world is phishing. In simple it refers to the practice of stealing data by sending in fake emails, texts, messages which appear to be legitimate thus inducing the person to put in the desired private information. This could in the form of a fake bank page or fake accounts on social media sites such as Instagram, Facebook, Twitter etc. This activity has heightened especially in social media platforms with many users in August 2019 being targeted with fake Instagram accounts in order to gain two-factor authentication.

4. Malware Sharing & Botnets

Malware or a malicious software has the ability to hack into the user data and steal information or private date in the form of spyware, can also extract money in case bank accounts being compromised by phishing attempts through net banking or use of bank webpage in the form of ransomware. Once a social media account is compromised i.e. a malware has been installed in the system it can then be used to send malicious links to friends and relatives of users, thus compromising their private data as well.

Along with malware sharing another pertinent threat to data privacy are automated bots. These bots look for specific search terms on social media platforms and automatically follow the targeted user. These bots being large in number tend to form a network called botnet which send the targeted users spam messages, emails and texts breaching their privacy once clicked upon.

<u>INTERNATIONAL LAWS ON DATA PRIVACY OF SOCIAL MEDIA</u>

I. Universal Declaration of Human Rights (UDHR)

The Universal Declaration of Human Rights was the first ever international statute to mention privacy issues as fundamental and basic right of every human being. Article 12 of the declaration states the following:

"No one shall be subjected to arbitrary interference with his privacy, family, home or correspondence, nor attacks upon his honors and reputation. Everyone has the right to protect against attacks. "

It also put forth 4 types of privacy they being physical privacy (of a particular individual and their residence), decisional privacy (of the family of the individual), dignity (of one's reputation) and informational privacy (of the data one shares using the internet and social media).5

II. The Right to Privacy in the Digital Age: Report of the Office of the United Nations High Commissioner for Human Rights, 2014

This report was established by the United Nations keeping in mind the rising threat to data privacy with the advent of internet and social media. It laid down certain guidelines and stated that irrespective of national laws across the globe the state will only be allowed to intervene with private data of individual citizens if it does not infringe the provisions of the convention. It also talked about judicial intervention and how it is necessary but not a one stop solution to privacy issues. Taking into note how judicial intervention and committees merely act as rubber-stamping processes, it held that enforcing privacy of individuals should be a constructive and combined aim of the judiciary, administration and legislature.6

<u>**DATA PRIVACY: THE WAY FORWARD**</u>

As we have already discussed how data privacy is at weak pedestal across the globe often ignored and taken advantage of by social media giants. There is a need for enforcement of strict laws at the earliest along with the proper awareness among people regarding privacy issues. Many laws are already in place such as the Information Technology Act, 2000 in India, Data Protection Act 2018 in United Kingdom, the Personal Information Protection and Electronic Documents Act (PIPEDA) in Canada and the Federal Trade Commission Act (FTC) in United States of America. All the laws have put down various guidelines in order to prevent breach of privacy. Most of them lay down necessary guidelines to ask for consent and permission of users and individuals before sharing their private data with any third-party. To protect the users from deceptive practices of companies and social media giants. Also enforcing penalties in case of breach of data privacy through a software, computer or a site. However, there are still various loopholes in the said legislations. They lack a proper procedure that would restrain the social media giants from sharing the private data with third parties many at times placed outside the jurisdiction of national laws itself i.e. when they are stored in a different country where privacy laws are lenient.

Although about 67% people in India7 and 34% people in Canada8 have a knowledge regarding privacy rules & regulations of the country about

70-80% of them are concerned about where their data is actually going and feel that they might be hacked anytime. 38% people in U.K feel that the scenario of data privacy laws have deteriorated over the past year. The need of the hour is to take certain steps to prevent possible privacy breach until stringent laws are put into place regarding the same. Some of the steps in my opinion are as follows:

i. Regularly change the passwords that you use for your account on any social media platform and make sure that you do not use the same password everywhere just for the sake of remembering it quickly as it can be really dangerous making your account liable to be compromised easily.

ii. Make sure you go through the terms of service of the apps you use at least once, now I agree it is a really tedious task but for now is the best alternative to having your privacy compromised, especially in case of unpaid apps or sites.

iii. Make sure to keep the location services or the GPS of your devices turned off unless it is completely necessary or you are using the maps. This is so because location and address act as an essential information for initiating phishing attempts and botnet attacks.

CASE LAWS

1) Facebook Cambridge Analytica Case

One of the most popular cases which brought the issue of Data Privacy to the forefront of world news. In this case fake app by the name of "This is your Digital Life" was created and the data of about 87 million Facebook users was leaked and collected by Cambridge Analytica which the analyzed it and help influence the opinions of people during the 2016 U.S elections. Aiding election campaigns of contestants such as Ted Cruz and Donald Trump. It also influenced the UK Leave Vote Campaign.9

2) K.S Puttaswamy v. UOI

The most important case of Right to Privacy in India when the Right to Privacy was enlisted as a fundamental right as a part of Article 21 of The Right to Life& Liberty. This formed the ground of laws on data privacy in India.

3) Digital Rights Ireland Ltd v. Minister for Communications Andrew Roberts

In Digital Rights Ireland Ltd v. Minister for Communications, the European Court of Justice found the EU Data Retention Directive, which required and rendered the retention of communications data for up to two years, to be incompatible and inconsistent with Articles 7 and 8 of the EU

Charter of Fundamental Rights, which talks about the right to private and family life and the protection of personal data.10

4) In re Warrant to search an email account controlled and maintained by Microsoft Corp. Case of District Court

In this case it was held that the State Government has a right to ask for enquiry of emails on the terms of national security from Microsoft Corp. It was held that the government has a right even if the information is stored outside the country as when it comes to digital access there isn't a lack of jurisdiction per se.11

<u>CONCLUSION</u>

Having had a glimpse of what exactly the data privacy issues of social media are and the laws pertaining to the same in various countries, it is integral to keep in mind the importance of data privacy in today's times. In a world filled with tech giants almost having a monopoly over the market, taking undue advantage of private data by sharing it with third part to earn money in the form of promotions and sponsorships it is imperative to take control and have knowledge of your own data following the very essence of data privacy. Although the laws are in place but as already discussed there are lacunas in the frameworks thus rendering social media accounts of internet users liable to compromise. Therefore, the need of the hour is to spread awareness regarding the threats of data privacy, keep in mind the laws already enforceable so that you can use them to your advantage and finally take certain steps at our own level to ensure that the data we share and have feeded on various social media accounts is in safe hands.

<u>Author's Bio</u>

Kartikey is a passionate and enthusiastic explorer of diverse law fields and tries to inculcate his knowledge in the form of writings. He aspires to spread awareness regarding the hidden and much concealed part of laws that provide the readers with a different perspective towards certain rules & regulations.

CHAPTER SIXTEEN

THE INDIRECT EFFECTS OF SOCIAL MEDIA ON THE INDIAN ECONOMY

Author: Gnanavell, III year of B.Com.,LL.B.(Hons.) from School of excellence in Law, The Tamil Nadu Dr. Ambedkar Law University , Chennai, Tamilnadu.

Abstract

This blog is an analysis of the Indirect Effects of Social Media on the Indian Economy. We can see as an overview that the social media has nowadays has a greater influence on the life of the every human being. It helped the people to connect easily and share things innovatively. Though it is good on one side, it is on other side making the people to get addictive and unproductive. Thus resulting in the indirect effect of our India's GDP.

KEY WORDS: Social media, GDP, Algorithms, Internet, Economic growth.

Introduction

Our Indian economy is a developing country for the past 10 to 20 years. Day by day the technology and advancement of techniques are increasing at a rapid growth rate. With the growth of population the consumption of Social media is also increasing slowly and consistently. The influence of social media is vast and wide nowadays. From the 5 year kid to 70 year old man everyone are fond of using social media and creating profiles on it to engage with people. The social media helps to share things with friends and others, which was a very tough and complex in olden times. In a small screen we can able to see whatever things that happened in any corner of the world .Thus the social media usage has nowadays become like a habit that evolved in our day to day life. In this article we will be seeing how the Social media indirectly affects the Indian economy.

The Growth of Social Media Applications in India: An Era

With the widespread availability of internet access, the number of social media users in India has been steadily increasing day by day. The Indian government through the Digital India initiative has also played a significant role in this expansion of Internet usage.

After the Introduction of JIO telecom services in India at 2016, where it offered free unlimited Internet service for every JIO sim users. This offer attracted majority people in India and made the users to buy the Sim at less rate and use the internet at an unlimited rate. From this point the average keypad mobile user started to switch to the smartphone user with abundant availability of internet.

The Indian people started to install the Social media Applications like YouTube, Twitter, Facebook, Instagram, TikTok etc.[i]These social media apps made the people to sit at one place and consume the content for many Hours. It made the people addictive to the apps and affecting the productivity and their work. As the technology increases on one side the Cybercrime rates also started to increase on other side. Thus this how the Social media apps of other countries started to enter into our Indian market with the advent of Internet.

How Social media affects India's GDP

According to research data people in wealthy countries spend lesser time on social media. But in our India we are obsessed over these lip sync and dance videos. Also the countries like china promote these crappy videos in the social media feed throughout the world through algorithms but when you use the same apps in china they have more intelligent content videos in the feed and that's something to think about. We can see that the European countries where social media is used less their GDP is way more than Asian countries where social media is used a lot and people are obsessed with it.

So how do such videosaffect our GDP by watching and getting addicted such content we are not getting smarter, in turn it affects our productivity and it affects our GDP as we are sitting like an idol and watching the videos in Tiktok , YouTube etc. On an average Indians spend 2.3 hours to 3 hours on social media everyday by watching short reels and videos in Social media applications.

The Major Social media apps in India are foreign based applications. They design the apps according to the human mentality to get addictive more and more they use. In such way through the advertisements in the middle of videos they generate a lot of income. Thus an individual's productive time is converted as money by these social media applications.

Increased Social Media Influence during Covid-19

In the year 2020, when India was gripped by the Covid-19 pandemic, many people turned to social media to gather information or express themselves by making videos, singing songs. This pandemic period made everyone to have mobile phones and laptops in their hands compulsory in the name of online classes, Meetings, Work from home and many more. Many people gained fame as well as defame through social media.As the number of people using social media increased, the internet community were also growing very wider and larger.

This has made the children as well as youngsters to get addicted to games, social media apps and porn. To say the bitter truth according to data the more than 40% of youngsters in our India are addicted to pornographic contents. This has increased as many are at home and lonely. Thus the social media has spoiled many young minds by making them addictive to these unwanted videos.

Social Media Active users in India

The number of active social media users in India stood at 330 million in 2019 and is expected to rise to 448 million by 2023. And Also 290 million active social media user access social media networks via mobile devices. Whereas the total number of Internet users in India has risen to 658 million, accounting for roughly 47% of the total population in India.

PLATFORM	ACTIVE USERS (IN MILLIONS)
Facebook	491.53
Instagram	503.37
MX TakaTak	153.97
Moj	151.34
Twitter	295.44

Income generation from Social media

Many of us would have a doubt that how social media apps are making money out of it. The Social media applications like Youtube, Instagram generates advertisements to the users and they collect the money for those ads from the companies. The Different Users may have different ads according to the algorithms. They show ads to the users accordingly what the user likes in nature by use of cookies. Cookies is a like a storage which shows the search and web data of the user. For example if you searched for a watch in chrome, the ads may show the watch advertisements whichever website you open in future time period. Cookies save your preference and your data.

The Social Media users also nowadays generating money from it. They create some Content videos and they earn money from it. For example an average youtuber uploads a video and earns money through the views of audience and the subscription amount. Nowadays earning from social media have become a trend. The general concept is more the views, likes the more the money. [iii]

Conclusion

The Social Media's power is so unjudgeable in nature. The Social media is more advantageous in nature. But still there are also some disadvantages in it like addictiveness, over usage, being unproductive and many more. Also the social media cuts the physical interactivity between the people and turns into introvert in future time period. The more serious issue is that many people used the power of social media to bully others. So everything is fine until the limit is crossed. Thus the social media apps will be useful if we use it in a wise way.